Colonial Mentality and the Destiny of Africa

Godfrey Mwakikagile

Colonial Mentality and the Destiny of Africa

First Edition

ISBN 978-9987-9978-2-4

African Renaissance Press
Dar es Salaam, Tanzania

To Africa

Morocco
Tunesia
Western Sahara
Algeria
Libya
Egypt
Mauritania
Mali
Niger
Chad
Sudan
Eritrea
Senegal
Gambia
Burkina Faso
Djibouti
Guinea-Bissau
Guinea
Nigeria
Ethiopia
Sierra Leone
Ivory Coast
Ghana
Central African Republic
South Sudan
Somalia
Liberya
Togo
Cameroon
Benin
EQ. Guinea
Gabon
Uganda
Kenya
Congo
Rwanda
Burundi
Dem. Rep. Congo
Tanzania
Angola
Malawi
Zambia
Mozambique
Zimbabwe
Namibia
Botswana
Swaziland
South Africa
Lesotho

Introduction

Part One:

**Chapter One:
The imperial image of Africans
before and after the invasion
and conquest of Africa**

**Chapter Two:
Precolonial Africa:
The way we lived
before the coming of Europeans**

**Chapter Three:
National integrity
versus foreign influence**

**Chapter Four:
Africa and the West**

**Chapter Five:
Conquest of the mind:
Our experience and destiny
as Africans**

Part Two:

**Colonial Mentality
and the Destiny of Africa**

Appendix:

**Berlin 1884:
Remembering the conference
that divided Africa**

Introduction

THIS WORK is about the destiny of Africa. It looks at our place in the world and in relation to our former imperial rulers who really never left us alone. They never left Africa and they never intend to leave us alone.

Even when they say they are helping us, providing us with economic or financial aid, they do so to promote their own interests.

The assistance they provide is usually tied to conditions or to something they want to get from us; be it trading with us, getting our resources for nothing, or spreading their influence over us in order to control us. And we end up losing all the time.

The industrialised nations which provide assistance, and members of the elite in African countries, especially those who benefit from investments and economic aid, talk a lot about how conditions have improved and continue to improve in our countries because of the assistance we have received and continue to receive from donor countries. What they don't talk about is the actual condition of the masses who constitute the vast majority of the people and the poor in our countries. Their condition has not improved; in many cases, it is much worse than before. Nothing has trickled down to the grassroots.

That is what structural adjustment programmes (SAPs) imposed on our countries by the International Monetary

Fund (IMF) and the World Bank as a condition for financial assistance from them have done to our people. These austerity measures are, ostensibly, intended to rejuvenate our economies by forcing our countries to focus on trade – with the industrialised nations on whom we so heavily depend to sell our commodities – while ignoring social services at the expense of the masses.

Other donors impose equally harsh conditions on us to get assistance from them.

That is what, in stark terms, globalisation means to the poor in our countries.

Economic aid from developed countries has not helped them. It has helped, and continues to help, the elite (who also steal much of it) more than it has the poor.

It also, in general, helps donor nations – our former colonial masters and other industrialised nations – more than it does recipients: poverty-stricken countries.

Economic assistance from the former imperial powers helps perpetuate neo-colonial control and dependency of their former colonies.

The best examples are in Francophone Africa, demonstrated by Ivory Coast, Senegal, Cameroon, Gabon, the Congo Republic (Congo-Brazzaville) and others.

Ivory Coast stands out among all the satellites in the French orbit in Francophone Africa as being the most proud of such ties to her former colonial masters, attributing her economic success – at the expense of political independence – to imperial benevolence.

In Anglophone Africa, Kenya is one of the best examples where the British still maintain a tight grip on the political and economic life and destiny of the country and have produced an elite of black Englishmen and black Englishwomen. Many Kenyans are very proud of being "very British" in their manners and and life styles unlike their brethren in neighbouring Tanzania which was also ruled by Britain.

That is one of the tragedies of being brainwashed, and

whitewashed, by our former colonial masters, with many Africans thinking they are more European than African.

There are other powers who never ruled us but who also want to control our destiny. They are the new imperial rulers aligned with our former colonial masters determined to control the destiny of Africa.

There are also emerging powers, mainly Asian, making inroads into Africa to secure and promote – at our expense – their own economic interests including acquiring vast expanses of territory in a number of African countries just as Western powers led by the United States do.

That is the same approach our former colonial rulers used when they first came to Africa to establish colonies, signing "treaties of friendship" with our traditional rulers to swindles us out of our land and minerals as well as other resources.

All that is happening because we are weak. Our weakness is the best weapon our enemies have used to conquer and subjugate us. And that is the same weapon they use today to control us.

When we were first conquered by Europeans, we were also conquered in the intellectual realm. Our conquerors provided an intellectual rationale for their "cultural superiority" and our "backwardness," touting Western civilisation as a demonstration and manifestation of their innate higher intelligence and sophistication. It was all for imperial glory.

They spread their influence across the continent, penetrating our minds, and tried to convince us that Europe was better than Africa in every conceivable way; therefore, Europeans were better than Africans. With our dark skin, and dark minds, we lived in darkness in the Dark Continent.

They brought us the light we so desperately needed to be enlightened and live as full human beings.

That is the lie we were told. And we believed it. They conquered our minds.

Many Africans still believe that lie.

The task for us now and in the future is it to wage a sustained campaign of liberation and self-defence on the intellectual level in the realm of ideas and in the practical sense to implement the ideas we generate to achieve mental emancipation and create a new African.

That is the only way we can take full control of our destiny.

It also means returning to our roots and reclaiming our true African heritage, identity, cultural and spiritual values, traditions and institutions without which a true African renaissance, hence genuine emancipation, is impossible.

This is my seventieth-first year, a milestone in the history of my life which is an integral part of the history of my home country, Tanzania, and of post-colonial Africa in general since I was a part of the younger generation who witnessed the end of colonial rule on our continent. But that was only the beginning of true liberation.

The struggle for African liberation in general started long before I was born. It started with the resistance of our ancestors against the European invasion of our continent. And it continues today.

People of my generation helped lay the foundation of the post-colonial states across the continent by providing some of the manpower needed for nation building and consolidating our independence. Most African countries had won independence by 1968. The seventies, when many people of my generation completed school, were therefore – together with the sixties, the decade of independence – a critical phase in the history of post-colonial Africa in terms of liberation, nation building and national reconstruction.

The seventies were also the decade when the struggle for liberation from white minority rule in the countries of southern Africa was most intense.

Although all countries on the continent are now free, having won formal independence from our colonial rulers, they are not really free.

It is for the current younger generation and others after us to carry on the struggle until Africa is truly free. But that will be only when it is united even if it is on regional basis. That is the only viable alternative to immediate continental unification which has remained an unattainable ideal since the euphoric sixties.

Without unity, prospects are bleak African countries will ever develop or even survive as stable political entities. And they will not be able to defend themselves against external aggression and internal sabotage.

When I entered my seventieth-first year, after my birthday on October 4th, I decided to add another part to this book, originally published as *Conquest of the Mind: Imperial subjugation of Africa*, and focus on the problem of colonial mentality so prevalent among millions of Africans decades after independence. Hence the new title, *Colonial Mentality and the Destiny of Africa*.

It is a subject I have also addressed in *Conquest of the Mind* but with more emphasis in this work to highlight the negative impact of colonial mentality on the destiny of our continent.

God bless Africa.

Part One

Chapter One:

The imperial image of Africans before and after the invasion and conquest of Africa

RELATIONS between Africa and Europe have been strained from the beginning when the two first came into contact with each other. It is Europeans who started all that.

When they first came to Africa, they literally saw themselves as entering a continent that belonged to nobody. The people who lived there were nothing; they did not even have a history in spite of their existence and having lived on the continent for thousands of years. That was the European perception and image of Africans deliberately distorted to suit European interests.

No society is static even if outsiders fail or are unable to comprehend its dynamics and understand the direction in which it is moving, as was indeed the case with Europeans in relation to Africa; its dynamic nature being properly understood only by those who live in that society. Failure to comprehend its nature and dynamics does not justify the claim that it has no history and that its people have contributed nothing to human civilisation.

Civilisation itself is relative. The civilisation Europeans brought to Africa, for which they claim credit and rightfully so, should also include not just its virtues but also its vices for which they should also rightfully and proudly claim credit. That includes the destruction of Africans lives, ways of life and whole societies and civilisations through the centuries in the name of "civilisation" as if they had a monopoly on virtue and morality. That is when they say our history began: The history of Europeans in Africa is African history. Before then, there was none.

Fortunately, not all of them believe that. But there are many who still do. That is why racism is one of the major problems of the twentieth-first century just as it has been in the past. And will continue to be one well into the next century and probably beyond; with Africans, black people in general, being routinely disparaged as human beings.

That has been an integral part of our history from the time we were conquered. That was when darkness descended on us, darkness of racial injustices perpetrated against us by our conquerors.

That was when a part of our own history stopped; stopped by our conquerors because we could no longer control our destiny.

We no longer had the freedom to move in the direction we wanted to move and in which we would have moved and do what we wanted to do. Instead, we took another route into the future, forced to do so by our conquerors and even at a pace dictated by them.

But it is an insult to Africans and a disservice to scholarship to argue that Africans had no history worth studying and that our history started when Europeans invaded our continent.

Europeans were not invited by Africans to come to Africa. They invited themselves. And they came with bad intentions.

They "stormed" ashore. And Africans were caught

unaware of this invasion which the invaders later tried to justifying as a "civilising" mission to the "savages" and "heathens" who inhabited the "Dark Continent."

Not only were Africans dark-skinned; they also lived in "darkness" because of their unfathomable ignorance about the rest of the world – about which, frankly speaking, Europeans themselves knew very little in spite of their adventures abroad, not by many of them but by only a few explorers and other adventurers including pirates.

The vast majority of them knew nothing about the rest of the world anymore than Africans did. We all lived in darkness about the rest of the world, just as the rest of the world did about us. We knew little about them and they knew little about us.

If this lack of knowledge is a sign of inferiority, then Africans don't have a monopoly of that. And if lack of knowledge of a people's history is a basis for sound judgement about their history, then European claims that Africans had no history simply proves that those who make those claims don't know anything about history or what history is.

Their preconceived notions about Africa and its people formed the basis of their knowledge about some of the most complex societies in the history of mankind which constituted the world's second-largest continent Dr. W.E.B. Du Bois described in the following terms in his book *The Negro*:

"Africa is at once the most romantic and the most tragic of continents. Its very names reveal its mystery and wide-reaching influence. It is the 'Ethiopia' of the Greek, the 'Kush' and 'Punt' of the Egyptian, and the Arabian 'Land of the Blacks.'

To modern Europe it is the 'Dark Continent' and 'Land of Contrasts'; in literature it is the seat of the Sphinx and the lotus eaters, the home of the dwarfs, gnomes, and pixies, and the refuge of the gods; in commerce it is the slave mart and the source of ivory, ebony, rubber, gold, and diamonds.

What other continent can rival in interest this Ancient of Days?

There are those, nevertheless, who would write universal history and leave out Africa. But how, asks Ratzel, can one leave out the land of Egypt and Carthage? And Frobenius declares that in future Africa must more and more be regarded as an integral part of the great movement of world history....

Primarily Africa is the Land of the Blacks. The world has always been familiar with black men, who represent one of the most ancient of human stocks....The medieval European world, developing under the favorable physical conditions of the north temperate zone, knew the black man chiefly as a legend or occasional curiosity, but still as a fellow man – an Othello or a Prester John or an Antar.

The modern world, in contrast, knows the Negro chiefly as a bond slave in the West Indies and America. Add to this the fact that the darker races in other parts of the world have, in the last four centuries, lagged behind the flying and even feverish footsteps of Europe, and we face to-day a widespread assumption throughout the dominant world that color is a mark of inferiority.

The result is that in writing of this, one of the most ancient, persistent, and widespread stocks of mankind, one faces astounding prejudice. That which may be assumed as true of white men must be proven beyond peradventure if it relates to Negroes. One who writes of the development of the Negro race must continually insist that he is writing of a normal human stock, and that whatever it is fair to predicate of the mass of human beings may be predicated of the Negro.

It is the silent refusal to do this which has led to so much false writing on Africa and of its inhabitants." – (W.E.B. Du Bois, *The Negro*, originally published in 1915, New York: Cosimo Classics, Inc., 2010, pp. 5, 6 – 7).

Our history as Africans stretches back to the beginning of humanity and civilisation. Africa is acknowledged as the cradle of mankind. Yet we were told by our conquerors that we not only did not have history known to Europeans and others and even to ourselves; we were also inferior to them – our inferiority being an integral part of our nature.

The question that arose but which was never answered by them was why their ignorance of our history made them superior to us.

We are the ones who know our history and about ourselves more than they know about us. The knowledge we have about ourselves, which does not and cannot be taught to us by outsiders, is vital to our identity and dignity as a people who are no less human than others despite professions to the contrary by those who place us in a different category simply because of who and what we are.

We don't need their approval, or the approval of anybody else, to be who and what we are just as they don't need our approval to be who and what they are.

Yet, right from the beginning when our conquerors came and conquered us, they arrogated to themselves the right to define us. That right is a myth. Their definition of who and what we are has not changed the reality of who and what we really are.

Yes, they conquered us. Yes, they ruled us. But the colonial era was no more than an interruption of our history which stretches back into antiquity. The conquest of Africa was not the beginning of our history but a temporary setback in our determination to control our destiny. It was an abrogation of our *natural* right to be free and to be what we want to be.

It was also a period of deliberate attempts to destroy our identity, not just to exploit us and our natural resources. And that included ignoring our history and instead writing the history of Europeans in Africa, and what they did to us, and calling it African history – as if it was about us while it was clearly about white people, how they lived, and what they did to us supposedly to help us when they were there to help themselves and their mother countries in Europe. It is strange that in some places where they did "their best" to help Africans, the people in those places responded violently; an expression of gratitude for the "benevolence" of our conquerors.

Pain always triggers a response, sometimes a violent one. Pain inflicted on Africans is no exception. Remember Mau Mau. Also, remember the Nandi how hard they fought against British occupation in Kenya.

In South Africa, the Xhosa fought a 100-year war against their European invaders.

The Zulu, also in South Africa, fought Europeans in some of the bloodiest wars in the history of Africa including one in which the British suffered their worst defeat since the Crimean war. That was at the Battle of Isandlwana in January 1879. It was also their first defeat in their wars against the Zulu.

There was the Battle of the Blood River, also in South Africa, in December 1838 when the Zulu, led by King Dingane, massacred the Boers who tried to take away their land. The Ncome River turned red from the blood of the Zulu warriors who were killed by their white invaders.

Those are just a few examples of armed resistance by Africans against alien occupation.

Punitive expeditions by groups of colonial soldiers – including conscripted blacks led by white officers – against "rebellious" tribes in many parts of Africa which did not want to submit to imperial rule were not uncommon even when many Africans had resigned to fate after their initial resistance against alien rule imposed on them by Europeans. They did not willingly accept colonial rule. And the reason is simple. It is not part of human nature to rejoice when you are conquered, dominated, subjugated and exploited. Africans were no exception then, they are no exception now.

Yet the "history" of Africa, written by colonial administrators and apologists for imperial rule, is replete with inaccuracies to bolster and justify claims that Africans welcomed their conquerors and were glad to be brought up under colonial tutelage in the name of "civilisation." The only "civilising influence" they came under was authoritarian rule which was imposed on them to achieve colonial objectives.

The countries our colonial rulers came from practised democracy. The leaders of those countries were accountable to their people. But when they colonised Africa, they formed governments and passed laws which did not allow our people to enjoy democracy. The distinction was clear; so were the reasons. As colonised people, Africans did not have any rights the colonial rulers and the white settlers were bound to respect.

Colonial governments were not only undemocratic; they were oppressive and repressive. African leaders who assumed power after the end of colonial rule inherited the same apparatus – oppressive laws and institutions used by the colonial rulers to subjugate and oppress Africans. In many cases, oppression under African leaders was even worse than it was under colonial rule.

This is not an attempt to absolve the colonial rulers of responsibility for establishing oppressive governments in Africa when African leaders themselves are also blamed for oppressing their own people. It is simply to point out the fact that colonial governments and institutions established by Europeans were deliberately intended to be oppressive and repressive because colonised people were not considered to be equal to their colonisers.

The colonial rulers also robbed Africans of the freedom they enjoyed in their traditional societies where they even had the power to control their traditional rulers and sanction them if they abused or exceeded their authority. They could not exercise that power over their colonial rulers. It is a subject I have addressed later in the book.

Not only did the colonial rulers have absolute power over the "natives" – they centralised power. And there was no higher authority to which the colonised could appeal to redress their grievances against their rulers from Europe;

They were the pioneers and relentless champions of centralisation of power – hence centralised governments – in Africa which our leaders inherited at independence and which they went on to use with ruthless efficiency to suppress dissent, ostensibly for the sake of national unity under fragile states, an argument that was justified in some cases, while in most it was used simply to neutralise the opposition however legitimate.

The Colonial Office – in London in the case of British colonies – responsible for colonial governments was useless to the colonised in terms of addressing their grievances against the colonial rulers. It played an effective role only when African leaders started to negotiate with the colonial power, in London, to transfer power to Africans when our countries were approaching independence and needed new constitutions to legitimise our rights and safeguard our sovereign status after our foreign rulers departed.

Centralisation of power by the colonial rulers also ignited ethnic rivalries. Some – in fact many – ethnic groups, or tribes, were left out. Leaders of the new African governments after the end of colonial rule came from only a few groups.

Not every ethnic group could be represented in the government when power was concentrated in the hands of only a few people, unlike in the past during the precolonial era when there was no central authority – over many tribes – and every ethnic group had its own leaders. In fact, many civil conflicts – not outright wars in all cases – across the continent during the post-colonial era have been sparked by the leaders because of their refusal to form inclusive governments. They refuse to include other ethnic groups and allow meaningful political participation for all their citizens on equal basis.

Power is monopolised by a few individuals, from a handful of ethnic ethnic groups, in the *same way* it was concentrated in the hands of a few administrators during colonial rule in the nation's capital and a few outposts.

To consolidate power, the colonial rulers also passed draconian laws, including the Preventive Detention Act, which future African leaders – of independent states – also used to suffocate dissent and legitimise oppression of their own people.

Colonialists even introduced prisons unheard of in traditional African societies which had more humane ways of dealing with criminals. But there some cases when mob justice was administered, with tragic consequences; something that cannot be justified even if it was in some traditional contexts.

The negative impact of colonial rule cannot be underestimated. It was devastating in many cases. And probably more than anything else, it dehumanised Africans, a horrendous tragedy that also played a major role in conquering the minds of many Africans.

Yet, for some inexplicable reason, our conquerors may have really believed that we were glad to be colonised and ruled by them. This attitude is rooted in their history, not in our history. It has to do with their perception of us as a people, how they see us versus them. The idea or assertion that Africans, black people, are equally entitled to freedom – as much as white people are – is anathema to them. This reminds me of what James Baldwin stated in his essay, "Fifth Avenue, Uptown," published in July 1960 in *Esquire*:

"Negroes want to be treated like men: a perfectly straightforward statement containing seven words. People who have mastered Kant, Hegel, Shakespeare, Marx, Freud and the Bible find this statement utterly

impenetrable....

It is a terrible, an inexorable, law that one cannot deny the humanity of another without diminishing one's own: in the face of one's victim, one sees oneself." – (James Baldwin, "Fifth Avenue, Uptown," published in July 1960 in *Esquire*; and in James Baldwin, *Nobody Knows My Name*, New York: Dial Press, 1961).

Our humanity has been questioned, and even denied, long before Europeans set foot on African soil; their judgement based purely on their imagination and tales of adventurers who knew nothing about the people they claimed they knew: us.

The imperial rulers and many white settlers had no regard, absolutely none, for the wellbeing of Africans.

Such disregard was a continental phenomenon even if the parallels were not exact; it was the same experience, and humiliation, nonetheless, be it in Tanganyika, Kenya, Guinea or Mali. As I state in my book *Africa and the West*:

"In all the African colonies, exploitation went hand in hand with degradation and brutality.

In the Congo under the Belgian King Leopold II, Belgians chopped off the hands and arms of Africans who did not collect enough rubber from the forest.

In Tanganyika, when it was German East Africa, Germans introduced forced labor and corporal punishment, virtually enslaving Africans, a practice which triggered the Maji Maji war of resistance from 1905 – 07 and covered almost half of the country. The uprising almost ended German rule which was saved only after reinforcements were rushed from Germany.

The French in West Africa also introduced forced labor.

Some of the leaders of independent Africa toiled in those labor camps. Madeira Keita, a native of Mali who was active in the politics of Guinea before it won independence in 1958 and collaborated closely with Sekou Toure in founding the Democratic Party of Guinea, was one of them.

In April 1959, he became Interior Minister of Mali, and in August 1960, he also became Minister of National Defense, holding two ministerial posts under President Modibo Keita. He related his experience as a conscripted laborer:

'Before 1945, there was a colonial regime with government by decree, the regime of the *indignat*.

The *indignat* form of government permitted the colonial administration to put Africans in prison without any trial. Sometimes you were put in prison for two weeks because you did not greet the administrator or the commander. You were happy enough if they did not throw stones at you or send you to a work camp, because there was also forced labor at that time.

In 1947, I met French journalists who were very surprised to learn that forced labor was nonvoluntary and not paid for. Transportation was not even covered; nor were food and lodging. The only thing that was covered was work.'

The conquest of Africa inexorably led to such brutality because its purpose was exploitation which has no room for compassion. It was an invasion we could very well have done without.

The baneful foreign influence Africa is still subjected to is a result of that invasion. And we are now inextricably linked with our former conquerors, for better or for worse, in an international system which accentuates inequalities and from which no part of humanity can extricate itself.

But the materialism of the West, which has found its way into Africa with devastating impact, must be counterbalanced with the spirituality and sense of sharing of the African which animates his culture, indeed his very being." – Godfrey Mwakikagile, *Africa and the West*, Huntington, New York: Nova Science Publishers, Inc., 2000, pp. 14 – 15; Madeira Keita, "Le Parti Unique en Afrique," in *Presence Africaine*, No. 30, February – March 1960; and Madeira Keita, "The Single Party in Africa," in Paul E. Sigmund, ed., *The Ideologies of the Developing Nations*, New York: Praeger, 1963, p. 170. On the African uprising and war of resistance against German colonial rule in Tanganyika, see, among other works, G. C. K. Gwassa and John Iliffe, eds., *Records of the Maji-Maji Rising*, Dar es Salaam: Tanzania Publishing House, 1968).

I also state in the same book:

"The argument that we blacks are genetically inferior to members of other races is nothing new. It is a stereotype rooted in Western intellectual tradition and has even been given "credibility" by some of the most eminent thinkers of the Western world including Immanuel Kant, Georg Hegel, David Hume, and Baron de Montesquieu. Some of them did not even consider blacks to be full human beings. As Montesquieu stated in *The Spirit of the Laws*:

'These creatures are all over black, and with such a flat nose, that they can scarcely be pitied. It is hardly to be believed that God, who is a wise Being, should place a soul, especially a good soul, in such a black, ugly body. The Negroes prefer a glass necklace to that gold which polite nations so highly value: can there be a greater proof of their wanting common sense? It is impossible for us to suppose these creatures to be men.'

The other philosophers were no less racist. According to Kant:

'The Negroes of Africa have received from nature no intelligence that rises above the foolish. The difference

24

between the two races (black and white) is thus a substantial one: it appears to be just as great in respect of the faculties of the mind as in color.'

Hume:

'I am apt to suspect the Negroes...to be naturally inferior to the whites. There never was any civilized nation of any other complexion than white, nor even any individual eminent in action or speculation. No ingenious manufactures among them, no arts, no sciences...Such a uniform and constant difference could not happen, in so many countries and ages, if nature had not made an original distinction betwixt these breeds of men.'

And according to Hegel:

'Africa...is no historical part of the world; it has no movement or development to exhibit.'

It is a sentiment echoed more than 100 years later in contemporary times by many people including British historian Arnold Toynbee who died in 1975. As he put it:

'The black races alone have not contributed positively to any civilization.'

And in the words of that great humanitarian Dr. Albert Schweitzer:

'The Negro is a child, and with children nothing can be done without the use of authority. We must, therefore, so arrange the circumstances of daily life that my natural authority can find expression. With regard to the Negroes, then, I have coined the formula: 'I am your brother, it is true, but your elder brother"...

The conquest of Africa led not only to oppression and exploitation, but also to denigration of her culture and indigenous institutions. Africans, at least a vary large number of them, were brainwashed into believing that they had no history they could be proud of; that all their customs and traditions were bad, and that even their languages were bad....

When Africa was conquered by the imperial powers, she was also conquered by ideas...as a very effective weapon for conquering other people by conquering their minds....

There is no other continent which is endowed with so much in terms of natural resources. But there is also no other continent where it has been so easy for foreigners to take what does not belong to them....

Because of the pervasive nature of Western influence, its negative impact has reached all parts of the world, including Africa where the devastation wrought is difficult to contain because of the underdeveloped nature of our economies, and also because of our inability to resist such penetration.

The sheer scope of such influence, as well as its negative attraction especially among the youth who are mesmerized by the glitter of the West, is mind-boggling and far beyond our capacity to resist it. That is especially the case in the cities which continue to attract millions of people in search of better – read, Western – life. It is a burden Africa cannot bear.

The West may have harnessed the forces of nature and pushed the frontiers of knowledge in many areas, from which Africa has indeed benefited as has the rest of the world. But Africa's contribution – material and spiritual as well as intellectual – to the growth of Western civilization has never been fully acknowledged. Nor has the destruction of African civilization by the West through imperial conquest. That is undoubtedly one of the saddest chapters in the history of relations between Africa and the

West. As Immanuel Kant, although a racist, conceded in one of his works *Eternal Peace and Other Essays*:

'If we compare the barbarian instances of inhospitality...with the inhuman behavior of the civilized, and especially the commercial, states of our continent, the injustice practiced by them even in their first contact with foreign lands and peoples fills us with horror; the mere visiting of such peoples being regarded by them as equivalent to a conquest...The Negro lands,...The Cape of Good Hope, etc., on being discovered, were treated as countries that belonged to nobody; for the aboriginal inhabitants were reckoned as nothing...And all this has been done by nations who make a great ado about their piety, and who, while drinking up iniquity like water, would have themselves regarded as the very elect of orthodox faith.'

Africa has yet to recover from the multiple wounds inflicted on her by this Western invasion. But there is a glimmer of hope. And that is traditional Africa. In spite of all the devastating blows our continent has sustained from the West, traditional Africa continues to be the continent's spiritual anchor and bedrock of our values without which we are no more than a dilapidated house shifting on quick sand. It is to traditional society that we must turn to save Africa from the West, and also save ourselves – from ourselves....Our future may lie in the past." – (G. Mwakikagile, *Africa and The West*, ibid., pp. vii – ix, vi, 208, 218).

If Africans don't do that, true African Renaissance is impossible. It is traditional Africa which defines who and what we are as a people and as an organic entity because it is the heart and soul, and essence, of our very being, but capable of coexistence with others on the basis of equality without necessarily leading to a higher synthesis of cultures at the expense of individual cultural identities.

Culture is a vital force and source of life for a nation. A nation without culture has no soul. It has no spiritual identity. And it has no vitality of its own as if it is a lifeless corporeal entity.

Racial superstition on the part of our imperial conquerors – their belief that they were superior to us in every conceivable way – played a major part in the denigration and even in the destruction of our cultures and way of life as Africans.

East Africans who were born and brought up during colonial rule had more direct experience with racism than West Africans did. That was because of the larger white population in East Africa. The region had significant settler communities, especially in Kenya, although smaller and fewer in Tanganyika.

Many Africans had bitter experience with the colonial rulers and the white settlers. The racial injustices perpetrated against them spanned the spectrum, covering all areas of life. Many whites even expressed doubts about the intelligence – and even common sense – of black people. As I state in *Africa and the West*:

"Colonialism, as a system of oppression and exploitation, not only continued to plunder Africa but sought to instill in the minds of Africans feelings of inferiority to justify such domination...This is just one example – what Colonel Ewart Grogan, the doyen of the white settlers in colonial Kenya and leader of the Kenya British Empire Party, said about Africans attending the renowned Makerere University College in Uganda:

'Just teaching a lot of stupid monkeys to dress up like Europeans. Won't do any good. Just cause a lot of discontent. They can never be like us, so better for them not to try.'

Another (Kenyan) settler in the 'Dark Continent' had this:

'I've actually got a farm hand who wears a tie – but the stupid bastard doesn't realize you don't wear a tie without a shirt!'

The implication is obvious. It is a sweeping indictment against all "native Africans" as a bunch of idiots.

Yet another one, Sir Godfrey Huggins, Prime Minister of Southern Rhodesia, acclaimed as a British liberal, shot point-blank at a press conference in London:

"It is time for the people in England to realize that the white man in Africa is not prepared and never will be prepared to accept the African as an equal, either socially or politically. Is there something in their chromosomes which makes them more backward and different from peoples living in the East and West?" – (Godfrey Mwakikagile, *Africa and the West*, ibid., pp. 9 - 10, 69; Colin M. Turnbull, *The Lonely African*, New York: Simon and Schuster, 1962, pp. 89, 21, 90, 97).

The total disregard for the rights and wellbeing of Africans – utter contempt for an entire people – was earlier demonstrated by the arrogance of the imperial powers when they met at the Berlin Conference_in 1885. The conference led to the partition of Africa and was one of the most tragic events in the history of imperial conquest of non-Europeans round the globe.

Africans were not consulted about their fate. They were not even represented at the conference. Yet it was their fate, and the fate of their continent, that was being discussed and determined by Europeans who decided to divide Africa among themselves as if Africans did not even exist.

This kind of arrogance and utter contempt for Africans

was also demonstrated and expressed in its crudest form in many ways including verbal abuse, torture and even inflicting humiliating punishment on full-grown black men in front of their wives and children as well as other people, some of whom even looked up to them as role models in society. They were subjected to corporal punishment at the hands of the white settlers some of whom were young enough to be their sons and even grandsons.

Shooting blacks was equated with shooting wild animals, as some white settlers in Kenya conceded, including those who had moved there from apartheid South Africa. It was equivalent to game hunting for sport but was also, symbolically, a way of getting rid of the black scourge, cleansing the land of members of the lesser breed, black natives, if they could.

What is known as land grab nowadays – taking or grabbing the land away from African peasants and giving it to foreign investors and corporations in this era of globalisation – was practised before, during colonial rule, in the interest of white settlers.

Such arbitrary seizure of land, depriving Africans of their only means of livelihood which was also equivalent to life insurance, was simply seen as a white man's right exercised at will in what had become the white man's possession under the tropical sun.

In my book *Nyerere and Africa: End of an Era*, I have given one example of this kind of imperial arrogance demonstrated by what happened to Tom Mboya_who, together with Oginga Odinga was one of the leaders of the Kenyan delegation to the constitutional talks in London in 1960 – Jomo Kenyatta was still in prison – when Kenya was approaching independence and the country had to have a new constitution to validate its sovereign status.

One of the luminaries of the African independence movement who also became Kenyatta's heir apparent after Kenya emerged from colonial rule, Mboya stated in his book *Freedom and After* that he was walking on a street in

London one day during the constitutional talks when he was stopped by an old English lady who asked him:

"Which one of our possessions do you come from?"

It was the height of imperial arrogance.

Many white settlers in Africa felt the same way; so did a significant number of their fellow countrymen back home in Europe. They really believed they owned our countries and we owned nothing or only what they allowed us to have. Some of them may even have believed they owned us because we were at their mercy.

This kind of arrogance and domination was based on some mysterious logic that, for some inexplicable reason, they were superior to us as human beings.

The British settlers in East Africa, especially in Kenya, even wanted to form a giant federation comprising the British-ruled territories in the region stretching from Kenya to Southern Rhodesia. It would have been turned into a bastion of white supremacy like apartheid South Africa and as Southern Rhodesia attempted to do.

The white settlers in Kenya even declared the colony to be a "white man's country" as if black people did not even exist there. It was a sentiment articulated by many white settlers. Ewart Grogan, the most outspoken leader of the white settlers in Kenya, was known for such imperial arrogance and raw-naked racism. As I state in *Africa and the West*:

"A man with a flair for controversy and an outspoken racist, Grogan described himself as 'the baddest and boldest of a bold bad gang.' He also gained notoriety for publicly flogging Africans in Nairobi. The settlers from South Africa also came 'with the racial prejudices of that country. Frederick Jackson, Sir Charles Eliot's Deputy Commissioner, told the Foreign Office that the Protectorate was becoming a country of 'nigger-' and game-shooters....

Colonel Ewart Grogan, a leader of the white settlers, bluntly stated: 'We Europeans have to go on ruling this country and rule it with iron discipline...If the whole of the Kikuyu land unit is reverted to the Crown, then every Kikuyu would know that our little queen was a great Bwana.'" – (G. Mwakikagile, ibid., pp. 97, 113; E. S. Grogan, in the *East African Standard*, Nairobi, Kenya, 12 November 1910; Elspeth Huxley, *White Man's Country*, Vol. I, London and New York: Macmillan, 1935, pp. 222 – 223, 261 – 262; George Padmdore, *Pan-Africanism or Communism?: The Coming Struggle for Africa*, London: Denis Dobson, 1956, pp. 255, 256).

The humanity of Africans and their lives meant absolutely nothing to many whites, even if not all. Such callousness was demonstrated by the injustices and indignities black people suffered under colonial rule whose legitimacy was derived from the "inferiority" of Africans; hence the right of Europeans to rule them which some whites even claimed had divine mandate. Therefore, the "inferiority" of black people was "permanent."

They would never catch up with or be equal to their masters who were "superior" to them. Dominating and humiliating them was simply an accepted way of life. It was also an integral part of the colonial system and facilitated domination of members of "the lesser breed" – black people.

Even African children sometimes witnessed their parents and other adults being insulted and humiliated by their colonial masters. It happened in Kenya; it also happened in my home country, Tanganyika, even when the countries were on the verge of independence; the fifties, when I was growing up, being one of the most critical periods in the history of colonial rule in Africa.

Those of us who grew up the fifties as school children also suffered injustices because of racial inequalities. The problem was compounded by inequities in the provision of funds and facilities for education. Only meagre resources were allocated to education for African children.

That was in sharp contrast with the amount of money spent on schools for European and Asian children. The school I attended was no exception in terms of resource allocation. It was also the dawn of a new era in the history of Tanganyika, the largest colonial territory in East Africa.

The fifties which was a decade that preceded independence was a transitional period. It symbolised the identity and partly shaped the thinking of those who grew up during that period as a product of both eras, colonial and post-colonial. They also served as a bridge between the two.

In my books, *Life in Tanganyika in The Fifties* and *Life under British Colonial Rule*, I have written about the political climate, race relations, incidents of racial injustice and other subjects to show how life was in colonial Tanganyika during that period from the perspective of colonial subjects who hardly had any rights in their own country ruled and dominated by whites. Africans were lowest in the racial hierarchy, with Asians and Arabs ranked next to whites. Race was the prime determinant.

It has also been the nature imperialism to place Africans deliberately in the sub-human category not only in terms of intellect but also in every other conceivable way; a characterisation that had a profound impact on the lives of many Africans even in terms of self-esteem.

There were Africans who really believed we were inferior to whites, socially and intellectually and may be even genetically, and that we deserved to be brought up under colonial tutelage.

That mentality persists even today among some of them, including those of the younger generation, because of our history as a conquered people which is used to justify our "inferior" status.

That was also the attitude of some white settlers even

in Tanganyika, placing Africans in the same category with dogs or other animals, especially monkeys, when I was growing up in the fifties.

That was the case even after independence in the early sixties.

Even members of other races, not just whites, have been equally condescending and outright racist towards blacks.

Many people of Asian origin – mostly Indian and Pakistani – and Arabs in Tanganyika, later Tanzania, also harboured racist views about black people. But they did not express them openly in a country where they were far outnumbered by blacks and whose destiny lay in the hands of the black majority.

Chapter Two:

Precolonial Africa:
The way we lived
before the coming of Europeans

THE Africa our ancestors knew no longer exists. And what is left of it is receding further and further into the past.

One good example of what we have lost is good governance – and government – and how it was exercised and conducted in the traditional context, especially in terms of making decisions based on consensus and on communal basis.

There is a sharp contrast between precolonial and colonial – as well as post-colonial – Africa in terms of how we lived then and how we live today; also in terms of how we were governed then and how we are governed today especially since the advent of colonial rule.

All African countries today are highly centralised states, with most of the power concentrated at the centre in the hands of only a few people, at the top, mainly at the national level and in the nation's capital. The people cannot fully participate in making decisions which affect their lives, and their country as a whole, under this form of government.

There is a need for decentralisation in order to give most of the power to the people at the local level so that they can manage their own affairs instead of waiting for orders from the top telling them what to do. It is the people themselves, not bureaucrats in the nation's capital hundreds of miles away, who know what is best for them. They also know who is bad for them as a decision maker.

If you are not a part of the people at the local level, you cannot know their problems. Therefore, you cannot know the right solutions to the problems they face regardless of how well-intentioned you are in trying to help them.

Giving more power to the people at the local level is very African. That is how our ancestors lived. This step into the past, back to our roots, can form a firm basis on which to reorganise our countries in our quest for peace and democracy, stability and progress.

Many African countries are wracked by civil wars, while the rest remain unstable, because of our failure, refusal and unwillingness to return to our roots.

But we must also admit that not every African traditional society was democratic before the coming of Europeans.

Here are some examples.

The Buganda kingdom in Uganda was a highly centralised state ruled by *kabaka* (king) who brooked no dissent.

The Zulu nation under Shaka was highly regimented. And the Hehe state under Chief Mkwawa in what is Tanzania today was highly autocratic and militarised.

Although militarised states were the most autocratic, they were also the most successful militarily. They were also highly united, even if such unity was short-lived as was indeed the case because of repression.

Partly because of the war against the Germans during the 1890s, Mkwawa used all kinds of coercive tactics to keep his people in line. He also proved to be a brilliant military strategist who confounded his enemies, a reputation which inspired awe and loyalty among his followers.

In June 1891, Emil von Zelewski, the commander of the Defence Force for the entire colony of German East Africa (Deutsch-Ostafrika), set out with three companies from the capital Dar es Salaam on a punitive expedition against the Hehe in the Southern Highlands. On 16 August, his force was ambushed and virtually annihilated. Zelewski himself was killed. The Hehe also captured three cannons and 300 rifles.

This stunning defeat seriously weakened the military strength of the Germans and was a severe blow to their prestige.

Governor Julius von Soden tried to intimidate the Hehe and other interior tribes into submission by establishing military posts in their areas even at the cost of weakening German control over the coastal districts, but nothing worked; at least not then. The Hehe proved to be the toughest among the tribes which fought the Germans in Tanganyika.

Mkwawa aroused the admiration of his tribal members through military victories against the Ngoni and the defeat of the Zelewski expedition.

The Ngoni were another tribe of fierce fighters. They migrated to what is now Tanzania from Natal in South Africa between 1820 and 1840.

Mkwawa's reputation for invincibility acquired from these military exploits enabled him, even after his fortified capital Kweringa had been captured, to weld his people into a defiant force of immense fortitude who continued to wage guerrilla warfare against the Germans for years.

Pitting his wits against the tactics of German officers trained in the European tradition, and many times skillfully penetrating through the tight net of soldiers and military posts formed around him and his loyal followers, he struck at weak spots in the enemy's lines to the very last, until he committed suicide in the bush rather than be captured and humiliated to see his people fall under alien rule.

Friends and foes alike, including his German enemies, acknowledged him as master of guerrilla warfare who outwitted them because of his unsurpassed military tactics.

The Germans even cut off his head and took his skull to Germany. A legend was born, fortified by the "myth" that the Germans took Mkwawa's head to study his brain and try to find out how a member of an "inferior" race could outwit members of a "superior" race that was highest in the racial hierarchy..

His skull was returned to Tanganyika in 1954 and was kept in the National Museum in Dar es Salaam, then the capital of Tanzania, until it was returned to the Hehe. It is in the Mkwawa Memorial Museaum in Kalenga, Mkwawa's former capital, near the town of Iringa.

But Mkwawa's success in welding his people into a cohesive bloc was also due to unorthodox coercive tactics which only enhanced his military stature. As O. F. Raum states:

"The German records of that time, written by soldiers in the field against the Hehe chief, speak with high praise of the loyalty of his warriors. Yet it is not difficult to show that he secured this loyalty by harsh rather than gentle methods.

He built upon a reputation of ferocity which made his subjects cringe before him in awe; he forced the men to follow him while the women were ordered to go into hiding in the bush; he had nobles who sided with the Germans assassinated and their wives mutilated, and threw suspicion on the reliability of Prince's Hehe followers by spreading rumours about them which tended to frighten them back to him...(Captain T. von Prince was a German who established a military station at Iringa in the Hehe country in August 1896 where Mkwawa was still waging guerrilla warfare against the colonialists).

Moreover, his successful guerrilla tactics added to the general insecurity of anyone who had come to the conclusion that the fight against the Germans was hopeless." – (O. F. Raum, "German East Africa: Changes in African Tribal Life Under German Administration 1892 – 1914," in Vincent Harlow, E. M. Chilver, and Alison Smith, eds., *History of East Africa*, Vol. II, Oxford: Oxford University Press, 1965, p. 181).

But even in these autocratic states, there was still some amount of freedom at the local level, unavailable in many African countries today, because the traditional rulers could not exercise full control over their people in different parts of their realm due to poor communications and lack of an extensive security network of enforcers and informers.

Glorifying everything in our past, which has become an article of faith in the Afrocentric school of thought, is racial chauvinism which is no better than the imperialist arrogance of our conquerors who espoused the doctrine of white supremacy. As Kwesi Wiredu, a Ghanaian and an eminent African philosopher who is a member of the Akan, a community of ethnic groups native to Ghana and parts of Ivory Cost, states in his book, *Philosophy and African Culture:*

"Our traditional society was deeply authoritarian. Hardly any premium was placed on curiosity or independence of thought.

Our traditional culture is famous for an abundance of proverbs…generally consisting of what elders said or are said to have said…At the base of them all is the unanalytical, unscientific cast of mind, probably the most basic and pervasive anachronism afflicting our society." – (Kwesi Wiredu, *Philosophy and African Culture*, Cambridge: Cambridge University Press, 1980, pp. 15, 28, and 48).

But most of them were decentralised, enabling the

people to enjoy a degree of freedom in the conduct of personal affairs and communal relations at the village level, even if they could not exercise independence of thought at the "imperial" court, especially in highly regimented societies.

Not all Africans enjoy that kind of freedom in African countries today, many of which are police states – some of them even employing Gestapo tactics – even if not constitutionally so.

It is also worth remembering that village meetings "under the big tree" to discuss issues affecting the community and resolve disputes were fairly common in most African societies. In most of them, everybody in the village was invited to attend. This was direct democracy under which even the "lowliest" member of society could voice his opinion. The most humble was equally heard as the most exalted.

In many others, the people sent their representatives to confer with the elders. This was representative democracy no different in principle from the parliamentary democracy "introduced" to us by Europeans. As one Nigerian writer, writing under the pen-name of Frank Niger, stated in his article "The New African Myths" in the African scholarly journal *Transition:*

"Sitting in a legislative assembly of two or more organized parties with paid Head of Government and Leader of the Opposition is certainly foreign to Africa. But not the idea of parties representing viewpoints on the one hand, and *organized* as pressure groups on the other.

The different clans and families within the traditional system were in fact embryonic groups of dissent, in character with the limited field of activity of traditional society." – (Frank Niger, "The New African Myths," in *Transition,* Vol. 4, No. 16, Kampala, Uganda, 1964, p. 17, cited by Ali A. Mazrui, *Towards a Pax Africana: A Study of Ideology and Ambition*, London: Weidenfeld &

Nicolson, 1968, p. 250. See also Willie E. Abraham, *The Mind of Africa*, London: Weidenfeld, 1962, p. 152).

Therefore there is ample evidence which shows that democracy is not new to Africa. It was not introduced to us. You cannot introduce something that already exists in a society in which you are "introducing" it. Democracy is as new to Africa as fire is to mankind. As Julius Nyerere put it:

"The African concept of democracy is similar to that of the ancient Greeks, from whose language the word 'democracy' originated. To the Greeks, democracy meant simply 'government by discussion among equals.' The people discussed, and when they reached agreement, the result was a 'people's decision.'
Mr. Guy Clutton-Brock, writing about Nyasaland describes traditional African democracy as follows:

'The elders sit under the big tree and talk until they agree.'

This 'talking until you agree' is the essential of the traditional African concept of democracy...
When a group of 100 equals have sat and talked together until they have agreed where to dig a well – and 'until they have agreed' implies that they have produced many conflicting arguments before eventually agreeing – they have practiced democracy...
Basically, democracy is government by discussion as opposed to government by force, and by discussion between the people or their chosen representatives, as opposed to a hereditary clique.
Under the tribal system, whether there was a chief or not, African society was a society of equals, and it conducted its business by discussion." – (Julius Nyerere, "One-Party Rule," in *Spearhead*, Dar es Salaam,

Tanganyika; and in Paul E. Sigmund, Jr., ed., *The Ideologies of the Developing Nations*, New York: Praeger, 1963, p. 197).

But this democratic way of life in our African traditional societies was profoundly affected when Europeans imposed alien rule on us.

From then on, the colonialists had the final say in the conduct of our affairs. And our struggle for independence was rooted in this very idea of democracy as a natural right we had enjoyed for centuries before the advent of colonial rule, and in the universal belief that we were entitled to freedom just like everybody else. As one African philosopher put it, a state of independence is a state of nature – and one to be "gained" only because it had been lost, certainly not as something new.

Therefore even after we were subdued by imperial might, there was always the hope that, in spite of all the odds against us given the technological superiority of our conquerors, one day, somehow by every means at our disposal, we would regain that independence. And there is abundant evidence across the continent that Africans never gave up. What happened in Tanganyika, including my tribal homeland of Nyakyusaland in the Southern Highlands of what is now southwestern Tanzania where I grew up, is just one example:

"Expressions of African antagonism to the whites are recorded from the beginning.

In 1898 a Kondeland (Nyakyusaland) prophet foretold the disappearance of the whites: the event was to be hastened by a sacrifice to which several chiefs sent animals.

The proud Gaya of Kavirondo (in Kenya) once rose because they had been told by a magician that they would die of smallpox if they did not chase out the whites.

In 1904 the impersonator of the Konde god, Mbasi,

announced at night: 'I, Mbasi, will chase the whites away. You need not stir. Already have I given the missionary's house a kick' – it had been struck by lightning – 'and driven him away!'

In 1907 the Zaramo (a tribe in the coastal region in and around Dar es Salaam, the capital of Tanganyika) greeted the plentiful rains with the words: 'Our God blesses us and punishes the whites!' for the railway line had been washed away.

These facts revealed that the Africans had never become reconciled to white rule...

The acquiescence of ruling houses in the curtailment of their powers (by whites) exposed them to the attack of rival claimants who asserted that they could restore the past.

In retrospect the time before the white man acquired the glamour of a Paradise Lost. Adverse experiences with the occupying power, which had to put down insubordination and could not prevent (but which in many cases also encouraged) the excesses of individuals, helped to keep the idea of independence alive." – (O. Fraum, "Changes in African Tribal Life," op. cit., pp. 181 – 182).

Unfortunately, when we regained our independence, most of our leaders were more interested in aping our former colonial masters than they were in building our young nations – created by the colonialists – on the basis of our traditional institutions which had worked for us so well in the past before the coming of Europeans. Therefore, there was no Paradise Regained, it was still Paradise Lost.

Although each African tribe had its own institutions and system of government, they also had a lot in common as they still do today: participatory democracy; a sense of sharing and communal obligation; the extended family; *ubuntu* – philosophically the same as *ujamaa* – we are an integral part of each other because we are one, my life is meaningless, and your life is meaningless, if we don't value each other.

Other important aspects of the African traditional way of life, besides grassroots democracy and people's justice through deliberation and mass participation in passing judgement, were respect for elders and a strong attachment to customs and traditions which formed the basis of government on democratic basis and regulated communal relations and personal conduct.

African customs and traditions were so strong that even after Africans learned how to read and write, they still saw no need to have written tribal constitutions to which they could turn as the final arbiter when disputes arose in the conduct of government affairs in their traditional societies. It was also these customs and traditions which formed the body of laws and code of ethics by which people lived.

Ethical conduct was intimately tied to the imperative need to help others, including strangers. For example, in our traditional Nyakyusa society, several Europeans were given shelter after being rescued from the Arabs – by a Nyakyusa army of 5,000 men – who held them under siege in Karonga, Nyasaland, during the North-End War of 1887 – 1889 between the Arabs and the Europeans.

The Nyakyusa also provided food to German missionaries who settled in our district in the early 1890s. In fact the missionaries would not even have been allowed to settle had it not been for the hospitality of our ancestors. One major missionary settlement was only two miles from our house. It was a German settlement whose main establishment was Kyimbila Moravian Church.

I also remember when I was growing up in Nyakyusaland how deeply rooted the sense of sharing and communal obligation was in our traditional society.

When a family wanted a house built quickly, the head of the family – invariably the husband or the eldest son if the father was dead – would ask other men in the village and set a date with them when they all would come and help him build the house, without pay, except for a large meal and some local beer.

He would do the same thing if he wanted a large piece of land tilled. All the men in the village whom he had asked for some help would bring their own hoes, till the land, and feast afterwards.

During the late 1950s, my own family was a beneficiary of such communal tilling we call *ndimilya* in my tribal language, Nyakyusa.

Such is the sense of communal living and obligation in our traditional Nyakyusa society – which is common in other African societies, only in different shades – that was also intimately linked to grassroots democracy at the village level; for, democracy entails social obligation to help fellow members of society based on the principle that we are all equal before the law – including unwritten African customary law – and, above all else, before God. And the reason is simple.

A truly democratic society is a society of equals which also helps the weak and the needy. But it can't be a society of equality if it does not equally value the lives and needs of all of its members; which African societies did and still do today, especially in the rural areas.

Even in towns, there are strong bonds of kinship, especially for members of the same extended family and even for people who are not related but who come from the same area.

Our traditional past is the best foundation on which we can build a strong foundation for our modern countries, almost all of which were created by Europeans. There was no Tanganyika before Europeans came.

There was no Nyasaland, no Mozambique, Northern and Southern Rhodesia, Gold Coast, Ivory Coast, Nigeria, Sierra Leone, Uganda, Senegal, Kenya, Guinea, Upper Volta, Sudan, Togo, Angola, Niger, Belgian Congo or any of the other countries on the continent formed by Europeans until our conquerors came, conquered us, and put us under the same imperial flag according to their wishes, forcing members of different ethnic groups, including enemies, to live together as citizens of the same country – which never existed in precolonial times.

Our conquerors disrupted our traditional societies, destroyed our traditional institutions and African ways of life in many fundamental respects although they did not succeed in destroying everything and even in some cases deliberately preserved some of our traditional institutions – such as chiefdom – to facilitate imperial rule.

Examples abound across the continent showing that our countries can best be served if we return to our roots. Unfortunately, concentration of power in the hands of only a few people through centralisation under the modern African state tends to suffocate traditional institutions in most African countries.

That is because the centralised state is dictatorial, insular, corrupt, and contemptuous of the African traditional way of life, being a product of our conquerors itself whom it tries to ape in their European ways. As Dr. Amos Sawyer, former President of Liberia, states in his book *The Emergence of Autocracy in Liberia: Tragedy and Challenge*:

"In thinking about reconstituting the African political order,…we need to investigate African social processes and traditional patterns critically as a starting point for the development of systems of governance for African societies…(They) have proven to be resilient (and) they constitute the shelters for survival and foundations for *de facto* patterns of order…This is precisely the meaning of Amilcar Cabral's advice to 'return to the source'….

The organization of a system of governance from the top down is as unnatural and illogical as building a house from the roof to the ground….

[We need to look at] how diverse local communities, societies, and groups organize themselves over time for the production, distribution, and consumption of goods and services, for the achievement of just, rule-ordered relationships, and for the general advancement of knowledge and artisanship.

Such an analysis would reveal how they cope with problems, devise solutions, order their social relationships, and create linkages with others.

These are the essential relationships embodied in any constitutional order." – ((Amos Sawyer, *The Emergence of Autocracy in Liberia: Tragedy and Challenge*, San Francisco, California: ICS Press, 1992, pp. 306, and 307. See also Amilcar Cabral, *Return to the Source: Selected Speeches* , New York: Monthly Review Press, 1973).

This is the micro-constitutional order, at the local as opposed to the national level, which has been ignored or is being deliberately suffocated by the centralised state – through mass regimentation – typical of all African countries today.

Yet it is this local community and its institutions which was the engine of survival and progress and the foundation of government – as well as peace and stability – through direct or participatory democracy in traditional African societies for centuries.

Most African societies existed as independent political entities led by different chiefs or some other kind of traditional leader – each with his own chiefdom or princedom or whatever entity – within the same tribe or ethnic group.

My ethnic group, or tribe, the Nyakyusa, is one such example.

There were also tribes or ethnic groups which, mainly through conquest by more powerful ones, collectively constituted empires and kingdoms, each of these large states being under one ruler.

However, it is important to emphasise that even these conquered tribes were semi-autonomous entities – in many cases even autonomous – in the sense that they were not ruled directly from the top by the dominant tribe.

They managed their own affairs, a degree of freedom which enabled them to enjoy democracy. Hardly any of them enjoy that today under highly centralised states so prevalent across Africa except in very few countries that are democratic.

Even in kingdoms composed of only one ethnic group such as the Buganda, Bunyoro and Ankole in Uganda; the Kongo kingdom of the Bakongo ethnic group in what is now the Democratic Republic of Congo (a misnomer) or Congo-Kinshasa, Congo-Brazzaville and Angola; the people in those kingdoms had their own local leaders, in their own villages and communities, who did not wait for orders from the imperial court on how to manage their own affairs; so did chief-less ethnic groups such as the Igbo of southeastern Nigeria.

This was self-government in which every member of the community participated directly at village meetings or through their representatives who consulted with their chiefs and council of elders.

All those institutions have now been pulverised, or paralysed, under the modern African state whose suffocation of dissent and centralisation of power is totally un-African – in an African continent; so is the practice by most African leaders of perpetuating themselves in office through rigged elections.

In traditional African societies, leaders – chiefs and other traditional rulers and even kings – who ignored the wishes of the people were unceremoniously drummed out of "office."

Three factors militated against the emergence of dictatorship in traditional African societies.

The first was love of liberty. Africans have always been fiercely proud of their independence and distinctive identity as members of particular ethnic groups. Many tribal wars, all of which have been erroneously attributed to primitive tribalism by outsiders including "experts" as well as by many educated Africans, were fought by different tribes to maintain their freedom and independence from other tribes encroaching on their territory.

Sheer hatred of other tribes for no reason other than that they were ethnically different has been overly exaggerated as the cause of tribal wars. It was more the distrust or fear of strangers than hatred *per se*, which triggered most of those conflicts, and it sprang from real causes.

There were tribes which invaded other tribes to subjugate and raid their territory for cows, women, and even for slaves among some tribes but not all. For example, my tribe, the Nyakyusa, did not have the institution of slavery; nor did they raid neighbouring tribes. Instead, they were content to stay in their valley (Nyakyusaland of Rungwe and Kyela districts in the Great Rift Valley) which was – and still is – well-endowed with fertile soil, abundance of rain and food crops, rivers and lakes.

Therefore not all African tribes were predators.

It should also be remembered that most African tribes welcomed strangers, the kind of hospitality which would have been impossible to find in African societies if tribalism was the paramount factor in determining relations between members of different ethnic groups. They even intermarried. And predatory tribes would not have been raiding other tribes for women if they wanted to have families only with members of their own tribe.

Even highly ethnocentric tribes such as the Maasai of Tanzania and Kenya sometimes married outside their tribe and ventured outside their territory not necessarily for predatory purposes but to settle.

The Maasai are a Nilotic ethnic group. Yet they sometimes intermarried with members of another "racial" stock, the so-called Bantu, a term now outmoded and more linguistic than racial; it is applied to collectively identify hundreds of different tribes south of the Sahara whose languages are similar.

The term simply means "people" – with variation in spelling in different Bantu languages including Kiswahili (Swahili). For example, *bandu* means people in my tribal Nyakyusa language, while in East Africa's lingua franca, Swahili, *watu* means "people."

In singular form, *mundu* means "person" in Nyakyusa, while in Swahili, it is *mtu*. Hence the term Bantu, since the rest of the so-called Bantu languages have similar terms, only with slight variations from one tribe to another.

In fact we never even called ourselves "Bantu" before the coming of Europeans and even after that. It was W. H. I. Bleek, a librarian of the British government of the Cape Colony in South Africa who coined the term "Bantu" in the 1850s, just as Afrikaners coined "Hottentot," a derogatory term applied to one of the indigenous ethnic groups in South Africa.

Like the Maasai, the Tutsi, another Nilotic tribe, also intermarried with the Bantu. They intermarried with the Hutu of Rwanda and Burundi and even adopted their language. As W.O. Henderson states in his chapter, "German East Africa: 1884 – 1918," in the *History of East Africa*:

"The direction of assimilation was not always from the weaker to the more powerful, as the example of the adoption of Bantu speech by the Hamitic (sic) Tusi shows....

Masai married to Bantu women did not consider it beneath their dignity to settle with their peasant-in-laws.

A few Masai (traditionally pastoralists owning large herds of cattle like the Tusi) even became traders, taking ivory on donkeys to the coast...(And) some Tusi owned no herds and had become agriculturalists." – (W. O. Henderson, "German East Africa," in Vincent Harlow, E.

M. Chilver, and Alison Smith, editors, *History of East Africa, Vol. II*, Oxford: Oxford University Press, 1965, pp. pp. 165, and 166).

Such tribal intermingling and assimilation, as well as the adoption of lifestyles of "inferior" tribes by "superior" ones, would not have been possible had Africans been as tribalistic and hostile to each other as they have always been portrayed to be.

It was the love of independence from other tribes whose domination they resented, as opposed to raw-naked tribalism, which was responsible for many of the tribal wars which have been fought through the centuries in Africa.

Even the ethnic conflict – which is also described as "racial," "Nilotic" versus "Bantu," although there are no such races – between the Hutu and the Tutsi in both Rwanda and Burundi has to do with domination and oppression of the Hutu by the Tutsi for hundreds of years: about four hundred.

The Hutu finally retaliated in Rwanda on an unprecedented scale, unleashing genocide against the minority but historically dominant Tutsi whom they almost wiped out when they killed about one million of them in three months, the fastest large-scale massacre in modern history, faster than Hitler killed the Jews.

But the Tutsi are now back on top in Rwanda, determined to stay in power.

As a minority group, they fear extermination, and for good reason. There are some Hutus, especially militants, who are just as determined to wipe them out and "send them back" where they came from, up the Nile, floating dead, headed north.

Yet it is a recipe for catastrophe. Conflict between the two groups can be averted through dynamic compromise.

The Hutu will never accept domination by the Tutsi, which they have endured for so long after they were conquered by them.

It is the same problem in Burundi, with the same ethnic composition and asymmetrical relationship.

The Hutu are a numerical majority but a political minority in terms of power in Rwanda ruled by the Tutsi-dominated Rwandan Patriotic Front (RPF). They were also a political minority, in spite of their numerical preponderance, in Burundi when the country was ruled and dominated by the Tutsi during much if its history.

The two countries will probably never know lasting peace unless they are split along ethnic lines into independent Hutu and Tutsi states, separate from each other – or until they agree to share power on the basis of proportional representation and guarantee security for the Tutsi minority.

To expect the Tutsi to agree to democracy on the basis of majority rule – one person one vote – is to expect them to commit suicide.

Democracy on the basis of majority rule is not only suicidal for the Tutsi; it will guarantee permanent domination of the Tutsi by the Hutu majority in both countries. And prospect are bleak the Hutu will agree to give up their democratic right of having power on the basis majority rule.

That is why splitting the two countries into Hutuland and Tutsiland may seem to be the only solution that will guarantee security and true democracy for both groups, regardless of how unrealistic it may be considering the fact that members of the two groups are so mixed that it will be impossible to separate them.

That is also the solution President Daniel arap Moi of Kenya publicly suggested, the first African president to do so. It is also one of the subjects I have addressed in some of my books, including *The Modern African State: Quest for Transformation*, *Military Coups in Africa Since the Sixties* and *Peace and Stability in Rwanda and Burundi: The Road Not Taken*.

The Tusi-Hutu conflict is a very important lesson for other African leaders and for the viability of the modern African state.

Such is the love of freedom and independence among Africans just like any other people. They will die for it, rather than be dominated by others including fellow Africans. As Dr. Kwame Nkrumah stated in his autobiography:

"It is far better to be free to govern or misgovern yourself than to be governed by anybody else." – ((Kwame Nkrumah, *Ghana: The Autobiography of Kwame Nkrumah*, New York: Thomas Nelson and sons, 1957; reprinted, Kwame Nkrumah, "Background to Independence," in Paul E. Sigmund, Jr., ed., *The Ideologies of the Developing Nations*, New York: Frederick A. Praeger, 1963, pp. 184 – 185).

African tribes who were invaded by other tribes – as well as by Arabs and Europeans at one time or another – resisted the invasions. Such wars of resistance against aggression by other tribes cannot be dismissed as a product of tribalism by "primitive" people who just love to fight. Few wars were fought – just because tribes hated each other.

Even conquering tribes did not always succeed in dominating weaker tribes. For example, the Ngoni of southern Tanzania conquered the Bena, their northern neighbours in the Southern Highlands. But they could not hold down their territory and impose their rule on them. They also conquered the Hehe, a tribe of formidable fighters in the same region of the Southern Highlands, only to be routed later.

They also penetrated Nyakyusaland, the home of another tribe of fierce fighters, only to be sent back fleeing.

The Ndebele, who also originally came from South

Africa like the Ngoni, conquered the Shona in what is Zimbabwe today. But they were never able to entirely subjugate them in spite of their formidable military skills and fierce reputation as fighters.

Some African tribes even formed alliances to resist aggression by stronger tribes; again it is worth remembering that such alliances would not have been possible if tribalism was the overriding factor in relations among different tribes.

Such alliances even led to the establishment of one government for all the allied ethnic groups who constituted multi-ethnic states no different from the multinational states of Europe.

One such alliance was the Fanti Confederation in the Gold Coast (now Ghana). As Kwame Nkrumah stated in his speech to the Gold Coast Legislative Assembly on the motion for independence on 10 July 1953 in which he also paid tribute to some of our African ancestors:

"We have travelled long distances from the days when our fathers came under alien subjugation to the present time….

Long even before her people had united into a nation, our ancestors had attained a great empire (the Ghana empire), which lasted until the eleventh century, when it fell before the attacks of the Moors of the North…

As with our enslaved brothers dragged from these shores to the Untied States and to the West Indies, throughout our tortuous history, we have not been docile under the heel of the conqueror….We constantly formed ourselves into cohesive blocs as a means of resistance against the alien force within our borders.

And so today we recall the birth of the Ashanti nation through Okomfo Anokye and Nana Osie Tutu and the symbolism entrenched in the Golden Stool (Hear! Hear! Hear!); the valiant wars against the British, the banishment of (Ashanti King) Nana Prempah the First to the

Seychelles Islands; the temporary disintegration of the (Ashanti) nation and its subsequent reunification....

Then the Fanti Confederation. The earliest manifestation of Gold Coast nationalism occurred in 1868 when Fanti Chiefs attempted to form the Fanti Confederation in order to defend themselves against the might of Ashanti and the incipient political encroachments of British merchants. It was also a union of the coastal states for mutual economic and social development. This was declared a dangerous conspiracy with the consequent arrest of its leaders (by the British)." – Kwame Nkrumah, "Nkrumah's Speech on the Motion for Independence," 10 July 1953, in George Padmore, *Pan-Africanism or Communism?: The Coming Struggle for Africa*, London: Dennis Dobson, 1956, Appendix III, pp. 405, 406, and 407).

But that did not extinguish the flame of independence burning in the hearts and souls of the Fanti and other Africans in the Gold Coast.

The Fanti live around Cape Coast and Elmina and are one of the Akan peoples. They speak a Twi language which is a part of the Kwa group.

But even after they formed a confederation to protect themselves against Ashanti incursions from the interior, several Fanti-Ashanti wars followed.

The Fanti were helped by the British who, nevertheless, destroyed the strong Fanti confederation established between 1868 and 1872, contending that it was a threat to their hegemonic control of the coast.

In 1874, a joint Fanti-British army defeated the Ashanti and, in the same year, the Fanti became an integral part of the British Gold Coast colony.

The Ashanti are also of Akan stock. They live in central Ghana.

Before the thirteenth century, Akan peoples migrated into the forest belt of present-day Ghana and established small states in the hilly country in the neighbourhood of modern Kumasi, the capital of the Ashanti or Asante region.

By the late seventeenth century, the states had been wielded by the Oyoko clan into the Ashanti confederation, with the capital at Kumasi and the Oyoko chieftain as king.

After subduing neighbouring states, the confederation came into conflict with the British settlements on the coast.

A series of Anglo-Ashanti wars in the nineteenth century culminated in the defeat of the confederation in 1896 – after one of the bloodiest wars (in 1891) in British colonial history – and in the annexation of Ashanti in 1901 to the British Gold Coast colony.

The British exiled the Ashanti king, Nana Prempah the First, to the Seychelles and broke up the confederation. It was restored in 1935.

In 1945 the Ashanti were given representation in the executive and legislative councils of the Gold Coast. They supported an unsuccessful attempt to give Ghana a federal constitution – under which there is more freedom – in 1954 and resisted the centralising measures taken by Nkrumah who was determined to establish a unitary state and succeeded in instituting one.

But their opposition to Nkrumah's unitary state, as well as the resistance by the Fanti confederation against Ashanti invasions, shows that all these people were determined to maintain their independence.

It is also important to remember that both groups, the Ashanti and the Fanti, did not have a unitary form of government but, instead, chose confederation. This form of government gave component units of the confederation, as well as individuals, more freedom to manage their own affairs more than they would have had even in a federation, let alone under a unitary state.

That is because the leaders knew that their people

would not accept living under mass regimentation and would even prefer a confederacy – an alliance of confederate states – to a confederation.

In Uganda, the kingdoms of Ankole, Buganda, Bunyoro, and Toro, and the princedom of Busoga, also resisted each other's encroachments, especially between Buganda and Bunyoro, the two main rivals.

During the sixteenth and seventeenth centuries, Bunyoro was the most powerful of the southern kingdoms, controlling an area that stretched into present-day Rwanda and Tanzania. But from around 1700, Buganda began to expand, largely at the expense of Bunyoro, and by 1800 it controlled a large territory bordering Lake Victoria from the Victoria Nile to the Kagera River which forms part of the Tanzania-Uganda border. It became the leading kingdom in the entire Uganda.

Buganda was centrally organised under *kabaka* (king) who maintained a large bureaucracy and a powerful army. But its concentration of power at the centre, Mengo Hill where the kabaka's palace and imperial court were located, became a liability. The kingdom could not expand any further because it could not maintain authoritarian control on the neighbouring people it tried to subjugate.

Had it been restructured on confederate basis to grant them autonomy, it is possible that it could have been a much larger and stable political entity extending beyond its ethnic base of the Baganda tribe, embracing several neighbouring ethnic groups.

Historically, Africans have resisted authoritarian rule preferring, instead, multiple centres of power under decentralised leadership.

Some ethnic groups which failed to resist encroachment by authoritarian rulers migrated to other parts of Africa rather than live under the subjugation of such despots. That is how the Ngoni came to Tanzania – they also settled in Nyasaland (now Malawi), Northern Rhodesia (renamed Zambia) and Mozambique– after they fled from Shaka in South Africa when he tried to forcibly incorporate them into his highly centralised Zulu nation.

Others who fled from him include the Ndebele who settled in what is Zimbabwe today; the Shangaan in Mozambique; and the Sotho, also known as the Sutu, who settled in Basutoland, what is now Lesotho.

The Sotho are the only ones who were able to form a nation or a national entity with clearly defined boundaries. And they have a rather different history from all the other groups who went in different directions after they left their home region of what became Natal province, now Kwazulu-Natal in post-apartheid South Africa.

Originally, the Sotho were members of different ethnic groups, remnants scattered during the disturbances, known as Mfecane, accompanying the rise of Shaka (1818 – 1828). They were rallied by Moshoeshoe, a commoner, into the Sotho nation.

A brilliant military tactician and diplomat, he not only defended his people from Zulu raids but also preserved their independence against the Boers and the British. He became the first king of the Basuto (Sotho) nation.

But he was not a tyrant like Shaka. That is why he was able to forge a nation out of many different tribes who fled from Shaka's tyranny. And that is why the people followed him willingly, transcending their tribal differences, to become one nation.

They valued their freedom and independence so much that they left their homelands and migrated to another part of southern Africa, in the Drakensberg Mountains, rather than submit to tyranny.

Such is the spirit of independence among Africans which militated against the institution of dictatorship in traditional African societies. And where tyranny was introduced, for example in the Zulu nation under Shaka, it did not last long. Shaka's reign lasted no more than 10 years. And he himself was assassinated by his own half-brother, Dingane.

In addition to love of liberty which checked authoritarianism in traditional African societies, another factor which militated against it was poor and even lack of, communications. This was especially the case over vast expanses of territory ruled by a paramount chief or a king. Such weak links with distant parts of the realm weakened control from the centre even for a leader with dictatorial tendencies.

But even such inclinations on his part were effectively checked by the people's ability to oust him from power. And it did happen.

Theoretically, African chiefs and other leaders ruled forever, since there were no elections in the Western sense of democracy. But in practice, African leaders stayed in power only as long as they fulfilled the wishes of the people. Otherwise they would be tossed out.

The third factor which blocked dictatorship from emerging in traditional Africa was rule by consensus. Traditional African rulers were more of listeners, or referees, than leaders because of the traditional system of checks and balances.

The leaders were led by the people and were there mainly to help maintain unity and hold the tribe or kingdom together by providing a rallying point the people could collectively identify with. They did not impose their will on the community or make final decisions.

They presided over deliberations – conducted by the council of their own advisers, or by the council of elders who represented the community, or by the entire community itself at a public village meeting everybody was free to attend and voice his/her opinion – in order to reach a consensus.

It was this government by unanimity, incorporating every viewpoint including that of an intransigent or hostile minority, which formed the essence of democracy in our traditional societies. No one was left out. All views were taken into account in reaching a consensus.

It is impossible to have government by the consent of the governed if it is not government by consensus.

Compromise was an essential component of African democracy. People sat down together and agreed on what they wanted to do or what they wanted to be done in their community.

That is how Africa was governed long before Europeans even considered invading our continent. And frankly speaking, this form of government by consensus – practiced by so-called "primitive, undemocratic" Africans – is more democratic than the Western-type of democracy under which the majority rule – even if they win only 51 percent of the vote – to the exclusion of others who are also an integral part of society.

How can such a society claim to be truly democratic when only some people – although a majority – who are not 100 percent of the population claim, and get, 100 percent of the power?

They control the government 100 percent. Yet the majority – their representatives whom they elected – don't speak for those who lost the election. In fact, in many cases, they don't even speak for the people who voted for them. They make decisions based on what they think is right, according to themselves, not necessarily according to the people who elected them to represent them.

Still, they claim they have the right to rule the people who did not even vote for them and form a government from which the minority are excluded; those who voted for the candidates who lost are the minority in this sense.

In traditional African societies, the system of governance did not exclude anyone from government because everybody was considered to be a part of the government. That form of government was the kind of government that was truly "government of the people, by the people, and for the people."

The people, not the leaders, were the government.

With a few exceptions such as Shaka and *kabaka* who

presided over highly centralised states, even kings bowed before the people, fulfilling their wishes and demands. They did not have or even claim absolute power or authority like most African leaders do today and whose imperial presidencies are hardly distinguishable from the state: "I am the state," reminiscent of Louis XIV, to whom the remark "L'etat c'est moi" – "I am the state" – is attributed.

Yoruba kings – known as *Oba* – in what is Nigeria and part of Benin today, whose history goes back hundreds of years, provide one good example of African potentates who, despite their high and venerable office, were men of the people nonetheless.

Even when Yoruba kings had to perform some brutal functions, it was always within the context of their culture – therefore the will of the people – which demanded that.

This is not to justify brutality but merely to emphasise that the kings were not absolute monarchs like many African dictators today who dispatch their opponents – real and imagined – to their graves at will. For example, when Benin and the adjacent kingdom of Dahomey were subject to the larger Yoruba empire of Oyo, the kings sacrificed hundreds of their subjects to tribal gods at annual festivals. The same ritual was performed in Oyo and in other Yoruba kingdoms in what is Nigeria today. But it was tribal religion, not imperial edicts, which demanded that. As Nigerian scholar E. Bolaji Idowu states in his book *Oludumare: God in Yoruba Belief*:

"The occasion was more often than not a matter of national or communal importance. There were divinities to whom the annual offering must be human. Such was Qramfe of Ile-Ife and of Ondo; so also was Ogun.

The sacrifice was also offered whenever it was believed expedient that someone should die as a sacrifice of appeasement in order that the community might be saved.

The victim of human sacrifice was usually made to bless the people in some prescribed way which bore upon the occasion of the sacrifice. He was then given a special message which he was to deliver on arrival in the presence of the Deity or the divinities….

In certain cases, a human who was sacrificed was more than just a victim offered to appease the divinities. He was believed to be going to represent the people before, and carry their petitions to, the higher power. Therefore, before the sacrifice, he was treated with reverence and accorded an extraordinary status.

Ironically enough, he was expected to put in every good word possible on behalf of those who offered him up. Because he was an ambassador, he was accompanied in the burial with certain things to be delivered with his message: those were things which were calculated to be efficacious in securing the pleasure of the divinities or the ancestors." – (E. Bolaji Idowu, *Oludumare: God in Yoruba Belief,* New York: Praeger, 1963, p. 199).

That was unquestionably barbaric. And this is an African condemning that. I am not a European or any other outsider with a penchant for denigrating everything African.

Let's just face it: some of our customs were bad, and this was one of them. There are others today which are also bad; for example, female genital mutilation and forcing little girls as young as 7, 8, and 9 years old to be married, as is the case in many tribes.

All that should be vehemently condemned by Africans themselves, and should be abolished.

But for those who relish such accounts in order to make fun of Africans and portray us as "savages," they should not forget that child abuse – rape, sodomy, pornography, torture and murder of children – is common even in "civilized" countries such as the United States and those of Europe.

They should also – and here is a remarkable contrast between the two practices (Yoruba versus Roman) in terms of intent and purpose – remember that:

"Roman spectators encouraged men to butcher each other, not under the influence of any cause so respectable as superstition, but from a morbid love of amusement at the sight of blood.

There were women among the spectators who sat and applauded. And with wild outcries urging the populace to refuse the petition of the kneeling gladiator, giving the signs of murder to the guards of the arena.

If the censurer of African customs read further and came down to the time when Christianity had taken possession of Southern Europe, he would observe that among the sportive recreations of highly cultivated Spanish Christians, was the shedding of blood, sometimes on behalf of Christianity; they would see a bull-fight in the list of amusements at Seville or an auto-da-fe in the square at Toledo." – (Edward Wilmot Blyden, *African Life and Customs*, London: C.M. Phillips, 1908, pp. 59 – 60).

That is Edward Wilmot Blyden in his book, *African Life and Customs,* published in 1908, showing that Europeans were no better than Africans and were, in fact, in many respects worse than Africans in their conduct.

Our critics, who call themselves Christian and civilised yet went on to enslave millions of Africans (true, with the help of some Africans), should be further reminded that more people "were thrown alive into the Atlantic by slave-ship captains, sacrificing to their god of profitability, than were ever beheaded by the kings of Dahomey or the Obas of Benin." – (Basil Davidson, *The African Slave Trade: Pre-colonial History 1450 – 1850*, Boston, USA: Little, Brown & Co., 1961, p. 244).

That is a British historian, Basil Davidson, not an

African like Blyden, saying that.

Even if Yoruba kings wanted to do what they did on their own, sacrifice or just kill some of their own people in an arrogant display of power, they would not have been able to do that without the approval of their subjects.

They are the ones who put and kept them in power. African kings were selected on the basis of character and their willingness to listen to advice as well as fulfill the needs of the people.

Look at Moshoeshoe, a commoner, who skillfully mobilised different tribes into the Sotho nation and became its first king because the people appreciated what he did.

Yoruba kings were selected by palace chiefs, and chiefs by the people. The Yoruba king, known as *Oni*, was selected from the royal patrilineal clan, the largest in the Yoruba spiritual centre: the city of Ife. Located in a farm region in southwestern Nigeria, Ife has a population of about 510,000.

The Yoruba are unique in Africa because of their tendency to form urban communities; and in their long history, they formed many city-states.

Many of the large cities in Nigeria today are in Yorubaland. They include Lagos, the largest city in the country and former federal capital; Ibadan, the largest indigenous city in black Africa and the second largest in Nigeria founded in the 1830s as a military camp during the Yoruba civil wars and developed into the most powerful Yoruba city-state; Abeokuta, a city of 450,000, founded in the 1830s by the Egba refugees from the Yoruba civil wars; and Ijebu-Ode, the capital of the Ijebu kingdom founded in the fifteenth century.

Long opposed to foreign contacts, the Ijebu kingdom remained closed to Europeans until 1892, when the British seized it in retaliation for the Ijebu's closing of trade routes to the north during the Yoruba civil wars.

All these and other cities are in southwestern Nigeria,

which is Yorubaland.

The old Yoruba kingdom of Oyo was traditionally one of the largest states in the entire West Africa. And according to Yoruba tradition, Ife is the oldest Yoruba town founded in 1300s A.D.

All Yoruba chiefs trace their descent from the first mythological ruler of Ife, Oduduwa, and they regard the reigning *Oni* (King) of Ife as their ritual superior.

Ife was the most powerful Yoruba kingdom until the late seventeenth century when Oyo surpassed it.

Yet in spite of all the power vested in the *Oni,* he could not rule as an absolute ruler, even if he had the means to do so, because of the spiritual role he played.

He was the link between his people and the departed ancestors. Therefore, he could not oppress his people without incurring the wrath of the ancestors; and he could not stay in office by alienating his people.

That was true of most African kings and other rulers on both counts.

Even a tyrannical ruler like Shaka could not make final decisions of vital national significance without consultation with, and the approval of, the *ibandla*, the supreme state council in the Zulu nation; nor could the chiefs in my tribal homeland, Nyakyusaland. The chief was a servant of the people, and not the other way around. As Simon Charsley states in his book, *The Princes of Nyakyusa*:

"The role itself was so lacking in institutionalised powers...The prince (chief) has no control over the appointment of those who would be his subordinates....

The...prince was certainly highly dependent upon his headmen, who, as the leaders of the people and largely chosen by them, were in a strong position vis-à-vis their prince.

Their power over their people might be minimal, yet at the same time, as the representatives of their people, over the prince their power could be considerable....

Mwakatungila was 'so humiliated by his councillors' that he retreated to the shelter of the (German Christian) mission....

The headmen might, it is said, even use violence against a recalcitrant prince; Mwankenja's father, Mwakipesile, is supposed to have been beaten into more submissive behaviour by his headmen....The important Mwangomo was tried by his own headmen and found at fault." – Simon R. Charsley, *The Princes of Nyakyusa*, Nairobi, Kenya: East African Publishing House, 1969, p. 69. See also Monica Wilson, *Communal Rituals of the Nyakyusa*, London: Oxford University Press, 1959).

But where in Africa today, under the modern African state, can a leader be tried and found at fault, or even be sanctioned by his peers or colleagues?

In our traditional societies before the coming of Europeans who created the countries and institutions that exist today across the continent, such arrogance of power by modern African leaders would, in many if not in most cases, have been unthinkable.

They would have been removed from "office."

That is what we need to do today: take a hard look at our traditional institutions which served us so well in the past and see what we can learn from them to make the modern African state more responsive to the needs and wishes of the people. That is democracy, which is nothing new to Africa; a phenomenon A. Merensky, a leader of the Berlin missionaries in Nyakyusaland, also observed so well in my homeland more than 100 years ago in 1891 – 92. Dictators were not tolerated:

"The chiefs of these people (the Nyakyusa) have no easy life. If they become old or behave in such a way that they lose favour with the people, their office is taken from them.

If a chief is quarrelsome, strikes people, or is miserly, slaughtering no cattle for the people and giving no presents to the councillors, then the Elders will come and remonstrate with him." – (A. Merensky, quoted by S.R. Charsley, *The Princes of Nyakyusa*, ibid., pp. 69 – 70).

The Nyakyusa also had other ways of disciplining their chiefs who did not act accordingly. One was by bringing them false news of an attack – and then telling them to fight alone when the chiefs tried to call their people to arms. Thus, the real dependence of the chiefs on their people could be brought forcibly and very effectively to their attention. And as Merensky goes on to explain the precarious position of any Nyakyusa chief:

"Or it may happen that the people really do forsake him in a family feud, and transfer their allegiance to the neighbouring enemy…The possibility of being deposed is ever-present for each chief." – (Merensky, ibid., p. 70).

So how were the Nyakyusa chiefs able to stay in power and retain their subjects?

One of the things I remember when I was growing up in Nyakyusaland is that we did not hear any complaints about the chiefs. It is not that the people did not speak up – they talked freely as they have all the time. There was no censorship, or even self-censorship for fear of reprisals, because there were no sanctions for airing your views or grievances as is the case today in most African countries. Just suggesting an alternative solution to problems invites swift retribution from the leaders; it is virtually tantamount to treason.

Freedom of speech was deeply rooted in Nyakyusa traditional society as everywhere else across the continent. What we usually heard was that the chiefs respected their subjects, and the people highly respected them in return.

Respect is earned, not forced. Fear is not respect. But

how often do you hear that about modern African leaders, that they are highly respected by their people? If you do, the sentiment is not genuine in most cases. That is because most Africans live in fear. If they criticise their leaders, the reward is swift punishment. Therefore there is no mutual respect between the leaders and their people.

But that is the solid foundation, mutual respect, upon which government was founded in traditional African societies; you don't respect someone whom you intimidate, dominate or oppress. It is an attribute even some outsiders who have studied African tribes – or ethnic groups – have noted. For example, in his study of the Nyakyusa during the late 1960s, Charsley states the following in answering to one fundamental question which has perplexed less-informed observers:

"Lacking any attractive or coercive force to monopolise (power and followers), how is it that the Nyakyusa princes (chiefs) attracted and retained their subjects?

The first and general answer is that they did so by fulfilling the general expectations of the good prince (chief). This involved behaving properly towards his headmen and people….

More specifically it was the obligation of hospitality that the Nyakuysa regarded as central. The prince (chief) should feed his people, and since food in general was not scarce, this meant primarily that he should provide them with beer, and, even more, with beef, the most prized of all foods.

The significance of this is not primarily nutritional; the Nyakyusa were well-fed as a rule, and with fish and milk available were probably not short of animal protein. Slaughtering for his people is, rather, significant as the expression *par excellence* of the relationship between prince and people." – (S.R. Charsley, ibid., pp. 71 and 95.See also Joseph Thomson, *To the Central African*

Lakes and Back, Vol. I, London, 1881, p. 267; Alison Smith, "The Southern Section of the Interior (of East Africa)," in Roland Oliver and Gervase Mathew, eds., *History of East Africa, Vol. I,* Oxford: Oxford University Press, 1961, pp. 258 – 259; Roland Oliver, "Discernible Developments in the Interior (of East Africa)," in Roland Oliver and Gervase Mathew, *History of East Africa, Vol. I.,* op cit., p. 209).

That is the kind of relationship which is sorely lacking today between most of the modern African leaders and their people. The people are afraid of them. And the leaders themselves are afraid of their own people.

There is no need to be afraid of your own people if you are doing the right thing and act accordingly.

In traditional African societies in general, the people were not afraid of their leaders – chiefs and others – except in a few cases such as Shaka, and Mwanga, the ruthless *kabaka* of the highly centralised kingdom of Buganda.

But such tyranny always worked against the tyrants. For example, in the case of Shaka, even some of his fellow Zulus fled from him, as did entire tribes when he tried to forcibly incorporate them into his Zulu empire which was one of the most centralised and autocratic on the entire continent.

When the people ran away from him, they were following the time-honoured African tradition of distrust of centralised power.

Even in small African tribes, the chiefs and other leaders pursued decentralisation almost with religious zeal in order to keep the tribe together. Their people deeply resented tyranny and would even break away under a different leader to go and settle elsewhere or fight back and depose – and even kill – their despotic rulers.

We have looked to outsiders for guidance for too long, only to end up as poor carbon copies of some of the worst these non-Africans have produced, instead of looking for the light that shines within.

African traditional institutions are light years ahead of all the -isms and other bankrupt and irrelevant ideas and ideologies we have imported from abroad – just to look "modern" and stupid.

In most fundamental respects, there is nothing wrong with the way we have lived for centuries before the coming of Europeans and other foreigners to our motherland. It may not be the best for the West, from whom we have copied almost everything in terms of governance and modernisation. And it may not be the best for the East from whom we imported another alien ideology, Marxism, when Karl Marx reigned supreme; although Marxism itself is Western in origin since Karl Marx was a Western thinker from Germany but his teachings were followed and practised in socialist and communist countries of Eastern Europe, especially in Russia and the Soviet Union as whole, more than anywhere else except China.

But the way we lived in precolonial times was and still is best for us. That is because Africa is neither East nor West, nor a hybrid of the two.

Our future is rooted in our past. We can learn from the rest of the world, as much as they can learn from us, without compromising our essence. There is nothing wrong with using a computer and remaining African to the marrow. But unless we return to our past for guidance, we will continue to drift aimlessly like a rudderless ship on the chartless sea.

Chapter Three:

National integrity
versus foreign influence

IT IS more than a cliché to say the world has shrunk. We live in a global village, thanks to mass communications and rapid travel across oceans and continents.

Diffusion of knowledge, the mass media, and air travel have brought distant cultures face to face; cultures which only a few years ago were as distant from each other as the stars. In fact, an African living in Accra, Abidjan, Lagos, Nairobi or Johannesburg today has more in common with a New Yorker or a Londoner than he does with a fellow African who lived centuries ago.

Who would have imagined that just within a generation, such diverse peoples as the indigenous peasants of the Andes mountains, the San in the Kalahari desert, the Hmong in the mountains of Laos, the Maasai on the plains of Serengeti, the Efiks in the Niger Delta, the Apache in the Arizona desert, would all one day come "face to face?" via television, videos, motion pictures, and the Internet?

What took Columbus and Vasco da Gama months to reach, now takes hours. Hop on a plane, you are on the other side of the world in the next few hours, and back. We no longer traverse vast expanse of territory, we telescope it. In other words, we shrink it.

When a Canadian cabinet member complained on Canadian national television in 1975 – I was a student in Detroit, Michigan, and saw the honourable minister on the news programme beamed across the border from Windsor – that his country was being culturally swamped by the United States, he didn't care the two nations had so much in common – "that's the problem," he would probably say – that they could pass for one country as an organically indivisible whole and no one would even notice the difference between the two.

Levelling a charge of what amounted to American cultural imperialism imposed on Canada, the cabinet member emphatically stated:

"Americans do not speak Swahili." – (Canadian cabinet minister, on Canadian Broadcasting Corporation (CBC), August 1975).

It would be almost impossible for Canadians to keep American influence out of Canada without resorting to some totalitarian measures. The two nations share a common border, a common language, in fact a common culture and even some history, making it impossible for Canada to insulate herself from her giant neighbour and things American. Who would want to erect stockades and jam broadcasts anyway? Communists tried it and ended up on the ash heap of history.

But there have always been attempts to insulate nations. For example, British political philosopher Edmund Burke defended prejudice as a defensive mechanism rooted in the traditions of society.

German philosopher Johann Herder contended that prejudice insulated nations from each other, enabling them to preserve their genuine identity.

But Herder neither saw nor advocated a hierarchy of nations. He respected all peoples and cultures and would today probably be acclaimed, or despised, as a precursor of multiculturalism.

He believed that authenticity alone, of a people's culture, was valuable. Those who came after him, and even some of his contemporaries, believed that some cultures are more authentic than others.

The Canadian minister's fear of his nation being "swamped" by American culture – hence his pointed remark, "Americans do not speak Swahili" – would undoubtedly have found sympathy in Herder. For, Herder not only believed that language was the essential attribute of each Volk; he approved the divisions of mankind resulting therefrom, because such linguistic fragmentation and isolation cut men from each other, forcing them into developing their own unique identities and cultures, thus protecting them from much of the corruption of national values and virtues as a result of foreign influence.

The fear of foreign influence is, in many cases, justified and no nationalist worth his salt would dismiss it lightly even today although we live in a global village. It has been an integral part of the history of mankind long before Burke, Herder, and Johann Fichte.

Fichte, in his *Addresses to the German Nation* he delivered as lectures at the University of Berlin, stated:

"Foreign cunning easily outmatched German simplicity and credulity." – (Johann Fichte, quoted by H. S. Reiss, *The Political Thought of the German Romantics, 1793 – 1815,* Oxford: Oxford University Press, 1955, p. 105).

He blamed Gallic cosmopolitanism and shared Herder's endorsement of prejudice as an insulation for maintaining national purity. But he did not share Herder's faith in its functional utility. Instead, he proposed in his work, *The Closed Commercial State,* stronger measures to insulate the nation from foreigners.

His concept of the nation as a manifestation of divine

order, combined with fanatical patriotism, stimulated German nationalism; in fact, his *Addresses to the German Nation* are noted for their morbid sensitivity typical of many fanatical patriots and intensely nationalistic individuals in different countries in all continents.

Fichte adopted from the French the doctrine that the world has been geographically constructed to accommodate nation-states as natural entities.

Giuseppe Mazzini said the same thing about his native land that when one looks at the geography of Italy, one can't help but notice that God had undoubtedly ordained it to be a nation with distinct natural boundaries.

Fichte expounded the concept in the following terms:

"Certain parts of the earth's surface, together with their inhabitants, are visibly destined by nature to form political entities." – (Fichte, ibid., p. 94).

The French were highly impressed by the utilitarian value of this doctrine, which they themselves had formulated, because their "natural" boundaries – the Pyrenees, the Alps, and the Rhine – enclosed a wider area than was actually inhabited by them. Mother Nature, in her inscrutable ways, seemed to have "endowed" the French with a large part of Germany.

The problem with Fichte's Fatherland was that Germans inhabited an area in central Europe which, as a plain land, was remarkable for its lack of distinctive features such as the "natural" frontiers of France and Italy's unmistakably "Italian" shape and landscape. So, where were the natural boundaries Fichte needed to give his Fatherland distinct identity besides the German language which he claimed was a language naturally structured to express the truth?

His ingenious solution, and profoundly philosophical answer, was to convert Herder's concept of cultural nationalism into a utilitarian doctrine of inner frontiers. As he put it:

"Those who speak the same language are linked together, before human intervention takes a hand, by mere nature with a host of invisible ties; they understand each other and are capable of communicating more and more closely with one another, they belong together, they are by nature one indivisible whole." – (Ibid., p. 7).

That is precisely the problem, at least in nationalist thinking. The "human intervention" Fichte talks about has already taken place, and it has internationalised man with English, French and other international languages including German, Fichte's "father tongue."

He himself decried Gallic cosmopolitanism for the woes that had befallen his Fatherland.

To smaller and weaker nations, a common language shared with a major power or powers is therefore a threat to their national identity and integrity. They are swamped by foreign ideas more than they swap ideas with foreigners; it is a one-way traffic and the flow is beyond their capacity to resist.

Not all foreign ideas are bad. Look at literacy, for example, and at technology imported by developing countries to facilitate economic development and improve living conditions, thanks mainly to Western civilisation. And if people have a strong culture, they have nothing to fear from such foreign "invasion."

Japan is a good example. She has absorbed Western technology and become an industrial power as well as an economic giant without compromising her essence and identity. She has remained essentially Japanese because of her strong culture.

But there are also bad ideas – bad influence – coming from foreigners. And small countries, in their small way, sometimes try to resist such intrusion.

If you stepped into Malawi during President Kamuzu

Banda's reign with long hair, tight clothes – or, for women, with a dress which did not cover the knees – chances were that you would be put out of the country on the next plane.

In Tanzania, especially during the sixties and seventies, a campaign was waged against miniskirts, tight trousers and shirts, skin-bleaching and other corrupting foreign influences including some music. Beauty contests were also banned.

Similar campaigns were waged in Zambia, Ethiopia, Congo-Kinshasa, Guinea and other African countries.

In promoting the cultural aspect of the revolution, Tanzania's ruling party (Tanganyika African National Union – TANU) decreed in August 1968:

"The highly reactionary and bourgeois practices such as beauty competitions [would be discontinued]. Beauty competitions do not in any way contribute to the transformation of the outlook of the women of Tanzania as required by the country's policies of socialism and self-reliance." – (Tanzania's ruling party (TANU), quoted by Colin Legum and John Drysdale, *Africa Contemporary Record: Annual Surveys and Documents 1968 – 1969*, London: Africa Research Limited, 1969, p. 215).

The TANU Youth League (TYL) also called for a ban on anything that symbolised the "cultural enslavement of the African" such as mini-skirts, tight jeans, and chemicals used to bleach skin and "dehumanize the African people." – (Ibid.).

The chairman of the TYL Central Committee, Mr. Lawi Nangwanda Sijaona, described members of the Youth League as "the shock troopers of socialist construction who are now being reconstituted in the avant-garde of the Tanzanian revolution." – (Lawi Nangwanda Sijaona, ibid.).

Is it xenophobia or paranoia?

Maybe there is legitimate reason to be paranoid especially when you have bad influence coming to you from all directions. But it is neither. It is not fear of all foreign influence but of bad influence, the kind Africa has been exposed to since the days of the ancient Greek mariners who first landed on the shores of East Africa during B.C. to trade, followed by Arabs who engaged in the diabolical traffic in human beings – enslaving Africans for centuries.

The coming of all those foreigners was an invasion, not an invitation, and Africa has not yet fully recovered from its devastating impact and probably never will.

It is that kind of foreign influence, bad influence, which is the bane of all civilisation. It perverts and corrodes the mind, erodes values, destroys identity; it dehumanises and even kills. It is an act of war which automatically triggers a response.

In a clash of cultures where one culture is more aggressive than the other, safety for the weaker lies in retreating into one's group.

In *Things Fall Apart,* Chinua Achebe best describes the situation in the African context where the people find solace in their traditional way of life although African laws no longer have the binding force they once had. They are not respected by the white man, thanks to foreign influence. The African way of life itself is not respected. Such has been the impact of foreign intrusion, a direct attack on the African personality.

Years later after the conquest of Africa, the African personality made a dramatic entry on the international scene in a highly symbolic way when Ghana's ambassador to the United Nations, later foreign minister, Alex Quaison-Sackey, became the first African to be elected president of the United Nations General Assembly on 1 December 1964, almost eight years after Ghana became the first black African country to win independence under the leadership of Kwame Nkrumah.

Quaison-Sackey regarded his election as the fulfillment of the African personality and as "a tribute to Africa…and to millions of people of African descent everywhere." – (Alex Quaison-Sackey, in his speech to the UN General Assembly, 1 December 1964, reported in *Ghanaian Times*, Accra, 2 – 4 December 1964. See also, Alex Quaison-Sackey, *Africa Unbound*, New York: Praeger Publishers, 1963, pp. 35 – 58).

In his book, *Africa Unbound*, Quaison-Sackey devotes an entire chapter to a discussion of the African personality which was subjugated under imperial rule as a result of foreign intrusion on a continental scale.

Such intrusion and subjugation of Africa had to be justified one way or another.

It was "justified" on scientific grounds based on some mysterious genetic logic that black people were innately inferior to members of other races and on the lowest rung of the evolutionary ladder.

Even today, the spread of foreign influence across Africa is rationalised in paternalistic terms as "the white man's burden," to use Kipling's phrase who himself was known for his imperialistic arrogance, because we Africans are, as Kwame Nkrumah pointed out, "still regarded as representing the infancy of mankind…Our highly sophisticated culture said to be simple and paralysed by inertia." – (Kwame Nkrumah, *Consciencism: Philosophy and Ideology for Decolonization and Development with Particular Reference to the African Revolution*, New York: Monthly Review Press, 1965, pp. 62 – 63).

Such paternalism towards Africans is more prevalent than it is towards anybody else and is even justified on moral grounds besides genetic. But it remains an invasion nonetheless. As renowned British scholar Margery Perham stated:

"European rule was imposed. The present generation of historians are writing a history of Africa and not only that of its invaders…

Presumed lack of any known history was formerly regarded as being one of the results of the innate inferiority of the Negro race, and the general concept of the darkness of the continent, and the darkness of the skins of its inhabitants, was extended to the condition of their minds…

European influence and government impinged upon the lives of Africans…(and) the colonial governments were essentially authoritarian…

The occupying powers fostered the introduction of powerful new ideas, both religious and political.

For the Africans there was certainly a price to pay. This cost has to be reckoned in terms of social dislocation and individual humiliation as the virtues of tribal life were impaired or destroyed.

Perhaps it is only with our recent experience of the force of African assertion and rejection of European power that we can measure the depth of the long-unseen social and psychological injuries which accompanied its obvious benefits. Some intimate evidence of the nature of these injuries comes from West Africa in the story appropriately entitled *Things Fall Apart*." – (Margery Perham, in Vincent Harlow, E.M. Chilver, and Alison Smith, eds., *History of East Africa, Vol. II*, Oxford: Oxford University Press, 1965, pp. xiii – xvi).

No people who have been subjected to such ridicule and contempt, and who have sustained such injuries, can take *any* foreign intrusion lightly. And that includes foreign influence, however benevolent; it is no less of an invasion, even without troops. Ideas are not spread by bullets, and the Bible was one of the most powerful weapons used, wrongly, to conquer Africa. As Jomo Kenyatta stated:

"The white man came and asked us to shut our eyes and pray. When we opened our eyes it was too late – our land was gone." – (Jomo Kenyatta, quoted by Ali A. Mzrui, *Towards a Pax Africana: A Study of Ideology and Ambition*, London: Weidenfeld & Nicolson, 1968, p. 198. See also Kenyatta, in *The Guardian*, Manchester, England, 30 January 1962, cited by A. Mazrui in *Towards a Pax Africana*; and Chinua Chebe, *Things Fall Apart*, London: Heinemann, 1958).

We ended up with the Bible and our European conquerors ended up with our land, became the lament across the continent.

The imperial mission itself, with all its brutalities, was justified on moral grounds. Even Christianity was inextricably linked with the exploitation of Africa and her people.

I remember when I was in secondary school, we were taught that Europeans came to Africa as benevolent saviours. They came to stop the slave trade. They brought us civilisation and material goods – we desperately needed – through commerce. Imperial conquest of Africa was based on what came to be known as the three Cs: Christianity, Commerce and Civilisation.

Thus, in African eyes, the white man assumed a moral posture he actually did not deserve and which did not correspond to reality: imperial conquest and exploitation of the continent. And he twisted the Scriptures to justify that on moral grounds.

So, when John Milton says the English – they were some of our conquerors – are God's chosen people, former colonial subjects including this writer from the former British territory of Tanganyika can't help but wonder the ease and consummate skill with which imperial rulers justified their conquest of Africa in fulfillment of their divine mission to rule members of the lesser breed on behalf of the Almighty.

But that is the imperial – not God's version. For, when Milton wrote his blank-verse *Paradise Lost,* detailing Lucifer's revolt against God and the fall of Adam and Eve in the Garden of Eden, which is indeed one of the masterpieces of English literature, dictating all his final great works – including *Paradise Lost, Paradise Regained, Samson Agonistes* – because he was totally blind by then; he wrote that not because he was the very elect of God as an Englishman but because he was just a writer, not even God's prophet.

All people are God's chosen people – because He chose to make them all.

Undaunted, our conquerors – in fact members of all "civilised nations" although not *all* members of civilised nations – maintained that they had the right to rule and even *define* members of "the lesser breed." As Sir Ivor Jennings put it when commenting on a people's right to self-determination:

"On the surface it seemed reasonable: let the people decide. It was in fact ridiculous because the people cannot decide until somebody decides who are the people." – (W. Ivor Jennings, *The Approach to Self-Government* Cambridge, United Kingdom: Cambridge University Press, 1956, p. 56).

As if the people themselves don't know who they are!

His imperial nation, Britain, arrogated to herself the right to define conquered people and arbitrarily compartmentalise them into Kenya, Rhodesia, Nyasaland, Bechuanaland, Nigeria, Gambia, Gold Coast, Sierra Leone, and the rest of her possessions she carved out for herself on the continent.

In response to the use of the distinctive appellation, "Gold Coast," Nkrumah stated in a speech to the Gold Coast National Assembly on 12 November 1956 shortly before he led his country to independence:

"The name Gold Coast is internationally regarded not as a name but as a description. It has therefore been the habit of each European country to give to the Gold Cost in its own language not the English title of 'Gold Coast,' but a name which in the language of that European country means 'gold coast.'

The Government consider it very undesirable that the Gold Cost should begin its independent international life with as many names as there are languages represented in the United Nations." – (Kwame Nkrumah, *I Speak of Freedom: A Statement of African Ideology*, New York: Praeger, 1961, p. 81).

It is a prerogative of the conqueror to define the conquered. But Nkrumah was saying in essence that it was time for us to define ourselves instead of being defined by others.

So, the Gold Cost emerged from colonial rule on 6 March 1957 as Ghana, as a continuation of the old empire of Ghana.

All across Africa, we did not just come into being on independence day; our existence as an organic entity on a continental scale, embodied in the African personality, preceded imperial rule. As Nkrumah stated in his national broadcast on the eve of the first conference of independent African states held in Accra in early 1958:

"For too long in our history, Africa has spoken through the voices of others. Now, what I have called the African personality in international affairs will have a chance of making its proper impact and will let the world know it through the voices of Africa's own sons." – (Ibid., p. 125).

But Africa cannot make her proper impact on the international scene as long as she remains under foreign domination and influence. Her interests are ignored, nobody pays any attention to what she says because she is divided and weak, unable to resist foreign influence and domination.

So what are we to do?

Foreign influence inexorably sweeps across national boundaries without the slightest concern for national integrity in a small world that is getting even smaller, thanks to mass communications, diffusion of knowledge, and an appetite for things foreign.

We can't insulate ourselves from foreign influence in this age. It is that diffuse. But there are ways to maintain national integrity without rejecting everything foreign. It is a distillation process.

Censorship is, more often than not, seen as a totalitarian weapon employed by despotic regimes in regimented societies to block the free flow of ideas in order to control the mind.

Foreign literature is banned, domestic cross-fertilisation of ideas is considered treason and always blamed on foreign intrigue.

And since conformity is synonymous with commitment under those regimes, a doctrine party ideologues openly espouse, anyone who deviates from the party line is a prime candidate for elimination. If he ends up in a mental institution for psychiatric attention on a menu of cathartic prescription to cleanse his mind, he's blessed. After years of "treatment," he comes out, that's if he makes it, as a zombie ready to toe the party line.

But in open societies also, for example in the United States where conservatism is synonymous with patriotism among ideologues on the Right and have liberals turning red at the implied notion that liberal orthodoxy is a threat to the nation's values, censorship is employed, although not as much as it is in regimented societies.

It is used, not to control the mind, but to keep it "clean." Yet totalitarian regimes claim they are doing the same thing, despite their notoriety for mass regimentation and intolerance of dissent. But because democratic societies also employ censorship, such curtailment of freedom impinges on individual liberty which is the very essence of democracy.

A question therefore arises: Is it better to force people to do what is morally right or leave them alone to do whatever they want to do including saturating their minds with what is considered to be morally reprehensible in open societies and what is considered subversive from an ideological standpoint articulated by doctrinaires in closed societies? After all, God gave man free will.

So, what is the moral justification for the employment of coercive tactics, banning some literature, for example, and forcing people not to read what they want to read? Freedom is sacred, but so is morality.

If there are degrees of morality, allowing people to exercise free will is morally superior to forcing them to do what is morally right because God says you are free to choose. It is a natural right.

But God also says don't destroy yourself, or others, while free societies say you can destroy yourself but not others. You even have the freedom to starve in democratic countries. If you don't want to work, you don't have to. You just won't have anything to live on, except beg. In regimented societies, it is virtually a crime not to work. There is work for everybody. Full employment is the Communist utopia, slaving for the state.

Yet both open and closed societies claim they are concerned with the long-term greatest good for the greatest number of their people. You don't have to be a statesman to have that concern. All you need is conscience. And if you have conscience, you can't be against censorship when it is employed in appropriate contexts but not arbitrarily.

Then when is censorship not censorship but statesmanship? When a nation is in danger. But who determines that a nation is in danger?

A ruling clique in a non-democratic society may claim that the nation is in danger because it is in danger of losing power and is trying to perpetuate itself in office.

In a democratic society, elected leaders may invent a foreign enemy to divert the attention of their restive population from domestic discontent.

Therefore, they all invoke patriotism, exhorting the people to be ready to die for the motherland, or fatherland, democratic or not. And millions have shed blood under the banner of dictatorship out of sheer patriotism.

Nations have always acknowledged the imperative need to defend their borders. A nation's armed forces usually fulfill that role besides hiring mercenaries or enlisting the help of allies.

But there is another form of defence which is just as critical to national survival. It is a sanitary cordon without which a nation can lose its identity and integrity, indeed its very being.

A nation without integrity is a nation without a spiritual personality. It is no more than just a crowd, an amorphous whole, devoid of meaning and identity derived from a distinct culture.

The Yoruba in Nigeria, for example, are known to have a rich cultural heritage going back for hundreds of years which helped to insulate them from negative foreign influence while they absorbed the best from the West without comprising their identity. Thus, when the British established their first protectorate in Nigeria, before anywhere else in the country, they found a people who were already well-insulated, culturally, and who had a glorious past no amount of foreign influence would be able to erase.

Other people in the area that came to be known as

Nigeria also had a rich cultural heritage, although – with a few exceptions – probably not as rich as that of the Yoruba who, despite their highly complex culture which insulated them from European influence, became some of the most highly educated people on the African continent, taking advantage of Western education while at the same time remaining Yoruba in all essential attributes as a people with their own identity and heritage.

Chief Anthony Enahoro, a Yoruba himself, telescoped such glorious past into this:

"Although Nigeria was the creation of European ambitions and rivalries, its peoples had their own ancient history before the arrival of the colonizers.

This new-created country contained…a number of great kingdoms which had evolved complex systems of government, independent of contact with Europe.

Within its frontiers were the great kingdoms of Bornu, with a known history of more than a thousand years; the Fulani Empire which had existed for a hundred years before its conquest by Britain; the Benin Empire, stretching at its zenith, from east of the Niger and to well beyond Nigeria's western borders; the Yoruba Empire of Oyo, which had once been one of the most powerful of the states of the Guinea Coast; the kingdoms of the Niger Delta and Calabar, the loosely organized Ibo peoples in the hinterland of the former Eastern Region, and the dukedoms and small tribes of the Plateau." – (Anthony Enahoro, in his statement to the Organisation of African Unity (O.A.U.) conference of African heads of state and government on the Nigerian civil war, Addis Ababa, Ethiopia, August 1968, in *Africa Contemporary Record*, op. cit., p. 672).

People in other parts of Africa have similar stories to tell about their glorious past, such as the empires of Ghana and Mali in West Africa; the kingdoms of Buganda and

Bunyoro in what is now Uganda in East Africa; Bakongo in some parts of what became Congo-Leopoldville, Congo-Brazzaville and Angola; the kingdoms of Zimbabwe, the Swazi, the Xhosa and the Zulu in Southern Africa. The list goes on and on.

It is a rich cultural heritage across the continent given concrete expression in the existence of the African personality as articulated by Dr. Nkrumah and other exponents of the Pan-African concept.

All those empires and kingdoms perished at the hands of foreign conquerors.

The ancient empire of Ghana in the savanna region of what is now eastern Senegal, southwestern Mali, and southern Mauritania, founded in the 500s A.D. by the Soninke people, was destroyed by the Almoravids – Berber Muslims – from Morocco who invaded it in 1076.

The medieval empire of Mali, one of the world's largest producers of gold, was also destroyed by Berbers whose empire, Songhai, founded in the 700s A.D. on the Middle Niger, was the largest of the empires in western Sudan.

The Ashanti kingdom, in Ghana today, was conquered by the British.

The kingdoms of Buganda and Bunyoro were also conquered by the British; so were the Zulu and the Xhosa.

The kingdom of Kongo, founded by the Bakongo, collapsed at the hands of the Portuguese enslaving Africans, a tragedy that befell the whole continent.

Therefore, one of the biggest culprits in the collapse of African empires and kingdoms and in the disintegration of African societies in general including less organised ones, was the slave trade which, unfortunately, was fuelled by Africans themselves in many cases.

But it was foreign invaders who attempted to deliver the fatal blow to the African personality. As Leopold Sedar Senghor stated in his speech at Oxford University on "Negritude":

"Paradoxically, it was the French who first forced us to seek its essence...when they enforced their policy of assimilation and thus deepened our despair....

Earlier, we had become aware within ourselves that assimilation was a failure; we could assimilate mathematics or the French language, but we could never strip off our black skins or root out black souls. And so we set out on a fervent quest for the 'holy grail': our collective soul. And we came upon it....

The early years of colonization and especially, even before colonization, the slave trade had ravaged black Africa like a bush fire, wiping out images and values in one vast carnage....

Negritude is the whole complex of civilized values – cultural, economic, social, and political – which characterize the black peoples, or, more precisely, the Negro-African world.

All these values are essentially informed by intuitive reason, because this sentient reason, the reason which comes to grips, expresses itself emotionally, through that self-surrender, that coalescence of subject and object; through myths, by which I mean the archetypal images of the collective soul; and, above all, through primordial rhythms, synchronized with those of the cosmos.

In other words, the sense of communion, the gift of mythmaking, the gift of rhythm, such are the essential elements of Negritude, which you will find indelibly stamped on all the works and activities of the black man." – (Leopold Sedar Senghor, in his speech "What is 'Negritude'?" at Oxford University, October 1961, published in *West Africa*, 4 November 1961. See also Senghor, "What is 'Negritude'?," in Paul E. Sigmund, ed., *The Ideologies of the Developing Nations*, New York: Praeger, 1963, pp. 248 – 249).

It is a sentiment shared by others across our vast and

embattled continent as a longing for our past as well as a celebration of the present. It is also a response to our collective humiliation at the hands of our conquerors whose rapacity is reviled in our collective psyche and conscience.

But although it was mainly foreign invaders who were responsible for the disintegration of African empires and kingdoms, and for the pollution of African cultures in their pristine beauty, not everything in our past was beautiful; nor is everything today. Genital mutilation is a good example. It is an abominable practice which has persisted for centuries in many African societies. And it needs to be stamped out – because of its cruelty and barbarism, and for health reasons, let alone for being a mortal danger – whatever its justification may be in the African cultural context.

And as we condemn our conquerors and glorify what is worthy of respect in our past and present, we must also acknowledge our folly in aiding and abetting that conquest. As Nnamdi Azikiwe stated in his speech to the conference of African heads of states and governments in Lagos, Nigeria, on 25 January 1962:

"Several empires and kingdoms flourished in Africa… These nations compared most favorably with their contemporaries in Europe and Asia…

These African empires and kingdoms disintegrated partly as a result of disunity created by fratricidal struggles for power and partly because of the slave trade.

Napata and Meroe are now ruins of an ancient civilization.

Ghanaa, Mali, Mellestine, Mossi, Songhay, and Bornu are now relics of a medieval civilization.

The Ashanti, Yoruba, Dahomey, Benin, and Hausa kingdoms are now objects of historical research.

Zimbabwe, Monomotapa, Zulu, and other kingdoms of East and Central Africa are now revered reminders of a historic past.

Brother fought against brother, and the slave trade depopulated the realms ruled by both. And Africa became a 'dark continent.'

In this process of acculturation through the centuries, this continent was pillaged, and its inhabitants were pilloried under a most brutal and ruthless form of oppression, ranging from slavery to colonialism." – (Nnamdi Azikiwe, "African Unity," speech delivered to the Lagos Conference of African heads of states and governments, Lagos, Nigeria, 25 January 1962. See also Azikiwe, "African Unity," in P. E. Sigmund, *The Ideologies of the Developing Nations*, op cit., p. 217).

Colonialism, as a system of oppression and exploitation, not only continued to plunder Africa but sought to instill in the minds of Africans feelings of inferiority to justify such domination and alienate them from their culture and heritage in order to turn them into objects of ridicule and contempt right on their own soil.

And the scorn and contempt for Africans by foreigners from all parts of the world including Asia, not just by Europeans and other people of European origin, has not stopped.

Therefore a vital part of our struggle against foreign domination, even today, has always been to explain and define positive aspects of our heritage and identity in order to affirm our humanity in a world where as an African people we are despised probably more than anybody else.

Automatically, our cultures and way of life as Africans – vibrant and positive cultures – become a weapon in defence of our collective "national" integrity of Africa – black Africa in particular – as an organic entity.

When, even some of the most enlightened among us, are despised just as much simply because of their black skin and black African roots regardless of their achievements which are even greater than the achievements of those who despise them, defence of the African personality becomes even more intensely "nationalistic" on behalf of black Africa as one "nation."

The kind of contempt which fuels such nationalism comes to mind when we recall numerous cases of racism and mistreatment of Africans by the colonial rulers and white settlers on the continent; some of them cited earlier. We were treated as if were nothing in our own motherland; not even as full human beings.

It is that kind of attitude which led to Mau Mau in Kenya where years earlier in 1905, the first British Governor, a retired soldier, General Sir Charles Eliot, after seizing the most fertile land from the "natives" in the central part of the country mostly inhabited by the Kikuyu, emphatically stated:

"The Protectorate is a White Man's Country. This being so, it is mere hypocrisy not to admit that white interests must be paramount and that the main object of our policy and legislation should be to found a white colony." – (Charles Eliot, quoted by George Padmore, *Pan-Africanism or Communism?: The Coming Struggle for Africa*, London: Denis Dobson, 1956, p. 233. See also Charles Eliot, *The East Africa Protectorate,* London: Arnold, 1905).

Those are not just tales from the colonial past; the same mentality still persists today and is shared by non-Africans, especially non-blacks, round the globe, putting black Africans constantly on the defensive about who and what they are. As Dr. Felix N. Okoye, a distinguished African scholar who was chairman of the Black Studies Department at the State University of New York at Brockport, stated when he wrote the book, *The American Image of Africa: Myth and Reality*:

"It is appropriate to recall the factors which prompted

me to undertake this historical investigation....

At dinner parties, I was shocked by the ethnocentrism of many highly educated Americans. University professors glibly described the peoples of the second largest continent as uncivilized, as savages. African religion and art were categorized as 'primitive.' Our dances were denounced as erotic.

The less sophisticated…repeatedly asked very annoying questions: Whether one began wearing clothes only after one's advent in their country, where was my spear, why no tribal markings on my face and no ring through my lips, how many lions I had as pets.

One professional bleeding heart was impudent enough to ask me whether it was true that Africans possessed tails!

The sponsors of the late shows on (American) television seemed to have an insatiable appetite for bwana-saying Africans and for the Tarzan balderdash. The movie commercials vociferously insisted that our continent was a land where animals had a sense of humor and where man alone was the stranger.

These are some of the unpleasantries African students in the United States are subjected to." – (Felix N. Okoye, *The American Image of Africa: Myth and Reality*, Buffalo, New York: Black Academy Press, 1971, p. 151. See also Walter Rodney, *How Europe Underdeveloped Africa*, Dar es Salaam, Tanzania: Tanzania Publishing House, 1973; and Walter Rodney, *The Groundings with My Brothers*, London: The Bogle-L'Ouverture Publications, 1969).

As an African student myself in the United States from the early to mid-seventies, I can testify to that, and much more.

But despised as we are round the globe, our identity is not what is at stake. We do have one and it is on the whole positive. It is our willingness to positively affirm it in a much larger context – beyond our territorial borders – that we should focus on. That is because Africa is one.

Yet we are so divided. But we are also united because of the similarities and the things we have in common in so many areas of life: similarities of kinship and marriage institutions, traditional political organisations, religious beliefs, and cosmological views shared by various civilisations of black Africa including our refusal to impose our traditional religions on other people.

All these similarities show that Africa forms an organic entity, variations within being branches of the same tree our invaders tried to cut down. Such similarities are a testament to the essence which is common to all black African societies uniting them as an organic whole. They cannot be explained any other way.

Thus, it is critical that our individual national identities and personalities – of Nigeria, Gambia, Tanzania, Liberia, Zambia, Namibia, Mali, Zimbabwe, Guinea, Mozambique, Togo, Rwanda, Lesotho, Ivory Coast, South Africa, Niger, Burkina Faso, Angola, Senegal, Congo, to name only a few – must be transcendent and exist only as parts, and vital components, of an indivisible whole which is Africa. And that entails collectively internalising our values, history and cultures in order to invigorate and sustain the African personality. They must, collectively, become an integral part of our nature.

An African child – since he is African first before he is Kenyan, Ghanaian, Malawian or Senegalese – must grow up knowing, as much as possible, about the Asantehene of Ghana, Chaka the Zulu, Mkwawa of Tanzania, Nkrumah, Nyerere, Sekou Toure, Kenyatta, Azikiwe, Lumumba, Lobengula, Queen Nzinga, Samori Ture, Haile Selassie, Maji Maji, Mau Mau, Oyo, Benin, the Shona, the Susu, the Fula, the Xhosa, as much as he knows about the leaders and the history of his/her own country.

He must know about the traditional laws and customs of as many African ethnic groups as possible – as much as he should his own. The African personality cannot be fully developed, and African culture cannot be sustained as a unifying force on a continental scale, without such systematic training.

Therefore the knowledge of the African child must be comprehensive, it must be continental. It cannot be limited to his/her territorial unit called Swaziland or Sierra Leone, Angola, Mali, Botswana or Togo. All those countries – and the rest on the continent – are artificial creations. Africa is not; it is a natural entity, an organic whole, whose personality is collectively embodied in all her people native to the continent including those in diaspora forcefully uprooted from their African motherland during the slave trade.

That Africans speak a common language of ideas, share philosophical conceptions of cosmic reality, is no accident. That there are striking similarities and common beliefs among people of diverse cultures across the continent, is not by sheer human contrivance.

When you have people from diverse cultures on such a vast continent with so much in common including linguistic similarities and practices such as elimination of the prefix in the last name among some groups in East and West Africa to denote feminine gender, common ancestry of black Africans seems to be the only plausible explanation; regardless of the diversity of cultures which evolved through the centuries as a result of migrations which necessitated adaptation to new environments.

Such evolution of different cultures and customs also reflects the nature of the new environments including geography where different groups moved to. For example, Mount Kenya would not have figured prominently in Kikuyu customs had there been no such mountain in the area where the Kikuyu settled.

Totally different peoples can originate from the same region and still have little in common: Asians, for example. Look at the Chinese and their neighbours, Indians in India.

Therefore the common elements shared by cultures

across Africa have nothing to do with the fact that Bantus of East, Central, and Southern Africa originated from West Africa about two thousand years ago. Common ancestry is the only explanation why they have so much in common including obvious racial characteristics, thus lending credibility to the concept of the African personality identified with a single entity, an indivisible whole, known as Africa or the African supra-nation or macron-nation of one people.

The imperial conquest of Africa not only subjugated that personality; it also distorted African history. As Nkrumah stated in his work *Consciencism*:

"The history of a nation is, unfortunately, too easily written as the history of its dominant class. But if the history of a nation, or a people, cannot be found in the history of a class, how much less can the history of a continent be found in what is not even a part of it – Europe.

Africa cannot be validly treated merely as the space in which Europe swelled up…Our history needs to be written as the history of our society, not as the story of European adventures.

African society must be treated as enjoying its own integrity; its history must be the mirror of that society and the European contact must find its place in this history only as an African experience, even if as a crucial one." – (Nkrumah, *Consciencism,* op. cit., p. 63).

Such distortion included teaching us that Europeans came to stop the slave trade. Yet those very same philanthropists became our conquerors when they used the Bible to pave the way for the colonisation of Africa. And the civilised nations they came from were the very ones which had fuelled and thrived on the slave trade, a fact they hardly mentioned.

They also talked about the "Arab Slave Trade" in East

Africa. But they never said the diabolical traffic in human beings on the other side of the continent was the "European Slave Trade." Instead, they ingeniously labelled it the "West African Slave Trade," a point underscored by Walter Rodney in his book *How Europe Underdeveloped Africa*:

"In East Africa and the Sudan, many Africans were taken by Arabs and were sold to Arab buyers. This is known – in European books – as the 'Arab Slave Trade.' Therefore, let it be clear that when Europeans shipped Africans to European buyers it was the 'European Slave trade' from Africa....

It is essential to recognise that the slave trade across the Atlantic Ocean was not the only connection which Europeans had with slaving in Africa.

The slave trade on the Indian Ocean has been called the 'East African slave trade' and the 'Arab slave trade' for so long that it hides the extent to which it was also a European slave trade.

When the slave trade from East Africa was at its height in the 18th century and in the early 19th century, the destination of most captives was the European-owned plantation economies of Mauritius, Réunion and Seychelles – as well as the Americas, via the Cape of Good Hope.

Besides, Africans labouring as slaves in certain Arab countries in the 18th and 19th centuries were all ultimately serving the European capitalist system which set up a demand for slave-grown products, such as the cloves grown in Zanzibar under the supervision of Arab masters."
– (Walter Rodney, *How Europe Underdeveloped Africa*, Dar es Salaam, Tanzania: Tanzania Publishing House, 1973, pp. 144 – 145, 146 – 147).

They also told us they came to stop tribal warfare. Yet they themselves ignited some of those conflicts, introduced the policy of "divide and rule," and even pitted converts of one Christian denomination against those of another as the French Catholics and the British Protestants did in Uganda, all for imperial glory, contrary to what they had come to preach. And they certainly never acknowledged how violent the civilised nations themselves were. As Kenyatta bitterly remarked:

"The European prides himself on having done a great service to the Africans by stopping the 'tribal warfares,' and says that the Africans ought to thank the strong power that has liberated them from their 'constant fear' of being attacked by the neighbouring warlike tribes.

But consider the difference between the method and motive employed in the so-called savage tribal warfares and those employed in the modern warfare waged by the 'civilized' tribes of Europe, and in which the Africans who have no part in the quarrels are forces to defend so-called democracy." – (Jomo Kenyatta, *Facing Mount Kenya*, London: Secker and Warburg, 1959, p. 212. The book was first published in 1938).

The African does not claim that his way of life is superior to those of other people– although most claim theirs are to his – but that it is the best for him while at the same time acknowledging his own shortcomings.

That is why he has shown a willingness to learn from other cultures, but not at wholesale expense of his; there are things he cherishes in his culture and which he will never give up.

The danger to African integrity comes not from learning from foreigners but when foreign influence perverts or tries to destroy values and other aspects of African culture Africans hold so dear.

Wholesale importation or indiscriminate acceptance of things foreign can pose a mortal danger to the African personality and to African identity itself.

In the face of such onslaught, selective censorship is the appropriate response, coupled with a sustained campaign to preserve and promote African culture as a defensive barrier against propagation of negative values from outside.

The best safeguard even when there is no palpable danger to national integrity is for Africans to proudly proclaim that there is nothing wrong with being African, and live accordingly, by hanging on – with bulldog tenacity – to the values they cherish.

There is much in our traditional way of life which is of value to us even today in this global village, something our conquerors never acknowledged anymore than other non-Africans have, a point underscored with magnificent eloquence by a Congolese villager in spite of his illiteracy. Yet, because of his Africanness, he is well-schooled in what it means to be an African. He has lived as one and intends to die as one:

"I have tried to understand the white man and his ways, but I can only see harm.

What happiness have they brought us?

They have given us a road we did not need, a road that brings more and more foreigners and enemies into our midst, causing trouble, making our women unclean, forcing us to a way of life that is not ours, planting crops we do not want, doing slave's work.

At least the BaNgwana left us with our beliefs, but the white man even wants to steal these from us.

He sends us missions to destroy our beliefs and to teach our children to recite fine-sounding words; but they are words we believe in anyway, most of them. And we live according to our beliefs, which is more than the white man does....

Let us live our way, because for us that is right....

I have looked at their way and do not like it, and I do not believe it is good for our people...

Perhaps the white man believes in his own way; if so, let him keep it, and let us keep ours, and let us both be men, not animals." – (Matungi, a Congolese villager, quoted by Colin Turnbull, *The Lonely African*, op. cit., pp. 81 – 82).

In spite of such provocation and injustice, the Congolese villager and his people remained pacifist. But the same intrusion provoked a totally different response from other subjugated Africans in the Belgian Congo as it did elsewhere in Africa.

Other Africans reacted the same way this villager and his people did in Congo. But there was no typical response, no particular pattern. The response to the European and Arab invaders varied from place to place. As the villager put it when he continued to lament his people's plight:

"The white man says we teach our children to hate the white man in our initiation schools. We do not. We merely teach them to believe, and to be men.

We are not like the Kitawala, for the Kitawala only exists to teach hatred of the white man, it teaches how to kill those who have tried to destroy our souls. It is not a good thing, but the white man brought it on himself.

In the old days there was the Anyota, and other beliefs like it, which killed in times of trouble. But it killed only one or two, and only until such time as the deaths made people realize that they were going against the ancestors. When they realized this, and behaved as they should, the trouble ended and the killings ended.

But the white man said the Anyota was evil, and the white man killed all the members he could find.

And so the white man brought about a trouble that could only be ended, in some people's minds, by killing the white man himself.

Our people do not believe like this, but we can

understand....

The white man has made it almost impossible for us to keep our beliefs, he makes us do bad things everyday…He forces us to plant the white man's cotton, to work for him on the roads, to treat him as though he were master of our souls as well as of our bodies....

I have tried to keep my dignity. I have tried to remain a man in the eyes of my father. Whatever I may have done with my body, I have never betrayed my beliefs with my mind." – (Ibid., pp. 82 – 83).

That is an authentic African speaking. That is the mind of Africa.

What this Congolese villager talks about, and laments on – that is the kind of price, and much worse, Africans had to pay for Western civilisation they had not even asked for.

But even if there were some benefits to Africans, was it worth it?

Would Africa have been better off without the white man and his civilisation?

Colonial rulers even waged "hidden" wars against Africans in different parts of the continent. They killed thousands and tens of thousands here and there. The wars – and the massacres – were never recorded in history. Here is one of them, according to a report, "Survivors Tell of France's 'Dirty War' in Cameroon Independence":

"It was a 'dirty war' waged by French colonial troops but it never made headlines and even today goes untold in school history books.

The brutal conflict unfolded in Cameroon, which on January 1 marks its 60th anniversary of independence -- the first of 17 African countries that became free from their colonial masters in 1960.

Many decades on, those who witnessed the violence recall events that shaped countless lives in the central

African country yet remain unchronicled today.

'My life was overturned,' Odile Mbouma, 72, said in the southwestern town of Ekite.

On the night of December 30, 1956, French troops arrived in the town and slaughtered dozens of people, perhaps as many as a hundred, she said.

'We were sitting under a tree when we suddenly heard the crackle of gunfire,' she said. 'It was everyone for themselves.'

Taking to her heels, the seven-year-old found herself jumping over bodies. 'They were everywhere.'

The troops were looking for independence fighters -- members of the Union of the Peoples of Cameroon (UPC), a nationalist movement established in 1948 that faced repression first by the French and later by Cameroonian soldiers.

French authorities labelled the UPC 'communist' and cracked down from 1955, driving the movement underground, though its charismatic founder Ruben Um Nyobe preached non-violence.

Buried in cement

In September 1958, Um Nyobe -- nicknamed Mpodol (for 'he who brings the word' in the Bassa language) -- was killed by French troops.

'His body was dragged around and displayed so that everybody (saw the corpse) of a man who was considered immortal,' said Louis Marie Mang, UPC activist in Eseka, where Um Nyobe is buried in a Protestant graveyard.

'To prevent traditional rites from being held, he was put in a block of cement and buried (without) a coffin.'

The conflict continued long beyond independence, for repression of the nationalists continued under Cameroon's first president, Ahmadou Ahidjo, who also banned public references to the UPC and to Um Nyobe.

The violence 'passed unnoticed, wiped from

memories,' according to Thomas Deltombe, Manuel Domergue and Jacob Tatsitsa, authors of *La guerre du Cameroun* (*Cameroon's War*), published in 2016.

They estimate that between 1955 and 1964, tens of thousands of people, including civilians as well as UPC members, were killed.

In Ekite, a wreath of flowers lies on the soil of a scrubland field at the end of a dirt track. 'The Nation will remember your sacrifice,' says a memorial notice.

'This is one of the mass graves where the nationalists were buried,' said Jean-Louis Kell, a UPC militant.

A second ditch was apparent a dozen metres (yards) away, and 'a third was discovered not long ago,' said Benoit Bassemel. He was seven during the French massacre and has tears in his eyes when he tells how his father was murdered.

'Free like the others'

UPC nationalists believe that the independence granted on January 1, 1960 was not what they fought for.

They view the country's two post-independence presidents, Ahidjo and Paul Biya, who has been in office since 1982, as working hand-in-hand with France.

'We wanted to be free like the other countries. We no longer wanted white people to subjugate us,' said 80-year-old Mathieu Njassep, in his tiny family apartment in Petit Paris, a poor district of Douala, the economic capital.

In 1960, aged 21, Njassep joined the Cameroon National Liberation Army (ALNK), the UPC's armed wing.

After two years of fighting, he was appointed secretary to Ernest Ouandie, a leading figure in the movement. He was sentenced to death but escaped the firing squad, unlike Ouandie, who was executed in 1971.

'We had almost nothing to wage a war with,' Njassep said.

'We carried out ambushes' with machetes, sticks and homemade guns. 'If we had had enough weapons, we would have beaten them.'

At the time, the ALNK had established its headquarters in the village of Bandenkop, on the land of the main western tribal group, the Bamileke. Fighting was fierce between the nationalists and the French army.

In the rugged valley from which ALNK commanders led operations, there is no sign of human life today and the only sound is that of a bubbling stream.

'This whole zone was regularly bombed' by the French air force, said Michel Eclador Pekoua, a former UPC official.

Pekoua and other nationalists say French planes dropped napalm. France has neither confirmed nor denied the use of the notorious incendiary weapon.

Decapitations

On a road 30 kilometres (19 miles) to the north, in Bafoussam, a roundabout is known as the 'crossroads of the guerrillas,' for it was where the decapitated heads of nationalists were placed on show, said Theophile Nono, head of a historical association, Memoire 60.

The regime's methods 'ranged from the arrest and arbitrary imprisonment of any Cameroonian suspected of 'rebellion' to systematic torture, with extrajudicial summary executions,' Nono said.

For many years the conflict mostly remained taboo in Cameroon. It was in the 1990s, when the authorities came under mounting pressure for democratic change, that people began to raise the historic past.

Biya, in a speech in 2010, paid tribute to 'people who dreamed of (independence), fought to obtain it and sacrificed their lives for it... Our people should be eternally grateful to them.'

After years of French silence, then president Francois

Hollande in 2015 became his country's first head of state to speak of 'a repression' of Cameroonian nationalists leading to 'tragic episodes.'

For many survivors, this is not enough.

'France must accept its responsibility,' Nono said.

'It must undertake to compensate victims of the dirty war, which has been carefully concealed by both the French side and the Cameroonian side.'" – (Reinnier Kaze, "Survivors Tell of France's 'Dirty War' in Cameroon Independence," AFP, Yahoo News!, 27 December 2019, *Humanitarian News*, 28 December 2019, *South Africa Today News*, 28 December 2019, *AllAfrica*, 28 December 2019, *Daily Mail*, London, 27 December 2019).

Even during the Mau Mau war of liberation, one of the most well-known insurgencies in colonial history anywhere in the world, the number of people who were killed was, deliberately, grossly underestimated by the British.

In Congo alone, when it was "owned" by King Leopold II as the Congo Free State, millions of people were killed in spite of his claim he was going to help improve the lives of the indigenous people.

Can the loss of millions of lives be justified, or can we say it was worth it, just to get some benefits of Western civilisation such as roads, schools and hospitals?

"Many people were killed by the colonial authorities in this region; in some parts hundreds and even thousands were killed. It happened throughout Africa. But the colonial rulers built schools and dispensaries and provided us with medicine to fight malaria and other diseases. Yes, we lost many people. But without the white man, we would not have what we have today: clothes, shoes, toothpaste, pens and pencils, paper, ink, soap, radios, sugar – the list goes on and on of the good things the white man brought to us."

Yes, he brought all that. He also killed millions of our

people – in Congo alone, probably ten million, and even chopped off hands and feet – and destroyed our traditional ways of life and institutions.

Yes, there were some benefits from Western civilisation. But would we not have been better off without all that and if we continued to live the way we did and chart our own way forward without any interference in our lives?

The answer is probably yes, considering the white man's motives for coming to Africa.

He should never have come to Africa with bad intentions: enslaving and exploiting the people and the land and all of its resources, taking over the whole continent as if it belonged to nobody, and turning Africans into strangers in their own homeland. As Nkrumah stated:

"The idea that when a handful of white settlers acquire a living space on our continent the indigenes must lose their right is…a serious travesty of justice....

I have always emphasized that Africa is not, and can never be, an extension of Europe." – (Nkrumah, in his speech to the UN General Assembly, 23 September 1960, quoted by Ali Mazrui, *Towards a Pax Africana*, op cit., pp. 14 –15).

But it was treated as one, as an appendage of Europe. Here is one example to illustrate the point. Before Kenya's independence Tom Mboya was once asked by an English lady on a street in London:

"Which one of our possessions do you come from?" – (Tom Mboya, *Freedom and After*, Oxford: Oxford University Press, 1963).

The French said Algeria was an integral part of France, a stupendous claim which triggered a response from Nkrumah that Africa was not and could never be an extension of Europe.

The Portuguese said Angola, Sao Tome & Principe, Mozambique, and Guinea-Bissau-Cape Verde were provinces of Portugal, prompting a sharp response from Julius Nyerere:

"Portugal pretends that her African colonies are really part of Europe, and that she abjures racial discrimination....The problem is that Portugal refuses to live in the twentieth century...She claims instead to be in the process of making European Gentlemen out of the African inhabitants of those areas, and talks proudly of the policy of equality for the 'assimilado.'

But Africans are not European, could not become European, and do not want to become European. They demand instead the right to be Africans in Africa, and to determine their own cultural, economic, and political future. This right is what Portugal denies....

The problem in this case is, therefore, how to wake up Portugal to the facts of politics in the modern day." – (Julius Nyerere, *Rhodesia in the Context of Southern Africa*, in *Foreign Affairs*, April 1966; reprinted in Nyerere, *Freedom and Socialism: Uhuru na Ujamaa; a Selection from Writings and Speeches, 1965 - 1967*, Dar es Salaam, Tanzania: Oxford University Press, 1968, pp. 145, 148).

We have our own identity as Africans. We cannot be turned into what we are not. We are what we are.

The task for us as Africans is to remain vigilant against evil forces bent on destroying the heart and soul of Africa.

That is especially the case in this era of globalisation which is again dominated by the West, as was the case during colonial rule, in what has virtually become a new form of imperialism in order to dominate and exploit us as if colonial rule never ended.

Globalisation is inherently unequal because of the

weakness of underdeveloped countries sharply contrasted with the might of the industrialised nations. The weakness of underdeveloped countries is clearly evident in the political, socioeconomic, technological and military arenas.

Globalisation is also inherently unequal, and is a destabilising force, because of the staggering inequalities which exist in many areas – including vast inequalities in the educational and health sectors and even in food production – between First World nations and Third World countries.

But it is also very important to understand that globalisation, or pulling Africa into the clutches of Western domination, is not really new; it is not a post-cold-war phenomenon or development.

The foundation and full expression of globalisation in the African context was colonialism and, before then, outright enslavement of millions of Africans whose labour was extracted to fuel the development and industrialisation of the Western world. Africa lost both material and human capital to the West for centuries.

The Arab slave trade in East Africa which went on for hundreds of years even before Europeans invaded and conquered Africa also devastated the region.

It was an era of ruthless exploitation of Africa's resources and her people. And the continent has not yet recovered from that brutal exploitation during some of the most tragic years in the history of imperialism.

The phenomenon itself, of imperialism, is as old as civilisation. It has its genesis in organised societies and their appetite for expansion. That is how empires start and that is how they are built. Empires are nothing new in human history.

Powerful people, societies or nations, have always conquered weaker ones, imposing their will – cultures, ideas and ways of life – on them.

The more advanced and sophisticated societies

became, the more aggressive and expansionist they became. It was mainly for material gain, but also for security and even purely for political ambitions competing with other societies or nations which pursued basically the same goals to secure their national interests, sometimes just for prestige.

The wellbeing of their victims, subjugated people such as Africans, was the last thing on their mind. They were an expendable commodity except for their cheap labour.

It was an imbalance of power, together with the injustices perpetrated against those who were conquered and subjugated, which played a major role in igniting and fuelling nationalist struggles for freedom and independence from alien rule and domination among the colonised.

And it was to be expected. Imperialism is by nature a predatory system. It is a system of inequalities with inherent biases against the people on whom it is imposed. Its practitioners operate from a position of strength, and superiority, treating the people they subjugate as inferior. This, in turn, causes feelings of alienation and low self-esteem among the colonised because of their mistreatment.

Everything which makes them what they are as a people – their cultures and entire ways of life – are described as inferior to those of the dominant group: their conquerors and imperial rulers.

Tragically, the victims themselves start to believe what they are taught by their conquerors; that they are indeed inferior to them – why not, they are their masters – and the cultures and ways of life of their imperial rulers are better than theirs, thus reinforcing feelings of inferiority and low self-esteem among the colonised.

They even start to believe there is nothing wrong with being colonised and that imperialism itself is a blessing; a powerful rationale for Western domination of much of the Third World even today.

Even Christianity was used in a perverted way to

subjugate and de-Africanise Africans – also to steal our land and minerals as well as other resources; its good message notwithstanding, propagated by genuine missionaries.

In fact, together with European explorers who preceded them, European missionaries paved the way for the colonisation of Africa and therefore played a major role in bringing Africans under imperial subjugation.

Conversion to Christianity amounted to Westernisation – acceptance of Western values, life styles and civilisation – just as Islamisation or conversion to Islam, which is taught only in Arabic, amounted to Arabisation and acceptance of Arab values, life styles and civilisation by African coverts; Islamisation being virtually equivalent to Arabisation in terms of culture. Hence acknowledgement of Islamisation as a way of life by the people themselves, including Africans, who have converted to Islam.

It is equally true of Christianisation as being almost equivalent to Westernisation or adoption of Western ways of life.

Acceptance of Christianity by Africans – just as acceptance of Islam – amounted to an abandonment and even a repudiation of African life styles and cultures although some of the teachings of these foreign religions were compatible with some aspects of African traditional ways of life; polygamy, which is accepted in Islam, being one good example.

In many – if not in most – cases, European missionaries themselves were not different from their brethren, European explorers and businessmen and other Europeans, in terms of perception of Africans as ignorant savages and inferior to whites who had brought light to the darkness of Africa.

Christianity – with missionaries intent on transforming the lives of the indigenous people and their traditional societies into something they were not – was a cultural imposition on Africans and even ignited conflicts among different African groups (so did Islam, waging Jihads to spread the faith and win converts), as was the case in Uganda and other parts of the continent.

Therefore its mission was not just religious – it was also cultural, hence imperial, and manifests itself even today as a form of cultural imperialism imposed on Africans by the West even when they convert to Christianity willingly; the results are the same, nonetheless, as a form of Western imperial influence and domination. For example, missionaries established schools, thus Westenising Africans, while at the same time converting them to an alien religion, at the expense of their identity.

That is one of the areas in which Africans are unique. Africans don't have a history of imposing their traditional religions or religious beliefs or any other values on other people, not even conquered ones who have fallen under the control of stronger tribes or ethnic groups. They are left with their own beliefs.

There are many things brought to Africa by Europeans which have not been entirely beneficial to the indigenous people. Some of them have been outright destructive, among them Western ways of life. And there is no question that we are still caught, and trapped, in the same clutches of Western domination as we were before the end of colonial rule.

One of the best examples of this domination is, of course, globalisation.

The elite in African countries and elsewhere in the Third World are among the biggest defenders of globalisation because they are the biggest beneficiaries of this new form of imperialism among Third Worlders.

It seems there is nothing we can do to reverse this condition. We are so weak that our enemies impose on us at will what we don't like. In many cases they do so surreptitiously, even though they don't have to, because of the control they have over us.

All that is done in order to destroy us. We must resist any kind of intrusion into Africa, and any kind of imposition on us the best way we can.

The first line of defence is maintaining our integrity as a people, distinct people, who are not trying to become what other people are.

We must remain what we are as a people, with our own identity, which is no less important – to us – than the identities of other people are to them. And that includes those who control us because they think, and even believe, that their way of life is better than ours – for us.

We are still trapped in the same predicament – as subjugated people – that was imposed on us by our conquerors centuries ago.

We are still subordinate to them even after the end colonial rule as they continue to dictate terms to us on what we should and should not do concerning our destiny.

There is no question that the coming of Europeans to Africa as conquerors changed the course of African history. It also changed the course of our destiny as a people. And it still has an impact on us today. We are not yet free.

That is because we don't have power. We cannot even protect ourselves and what belongs to us. Foreigners exploit Africa, and take whatever they want to take from us and out of the continent as if we don't even exist and everything in Africa belongs to them.

It all started with the conquest of Africa by the West.

Chapter Four:

Africa and the West

The destiny of Africa has been profoundly affected by what our conquerors from Europe decided to do to us when they first came to our motherland.

It is imperative that we look at Africa's place in the world especially in relation to the West because that is where our conquerors came from.

This critical analysis is as much an indictment of our conquerors as it is a self-examination of our own African personality whose integrity and destiny has been profoundly affected because of our lack of power.

That is how we were conquered in the first place, losing the whole continent to a mere handful of European soldiers and adventurers. And history may repeat itself unless we do something now for posterity. Otherwise we are going to remain sitting ducks, fair game for anybody who wants to take a shot at us. As Dr. Kwame Nkrumah stated in *Dark Days in Ghana*:

"While we remain divided, no single progressive independent African state is safe. The continent is disunited and powerless in world affairs." – (Kwame Nkrumah, *Dark Days in Ghana*, London: Panaf Publishers, 1969. See also Nkrumah, *Africa Must Unite*,

New York: Praeger, 1963, *Neo-Colonialism: The Last Stage of Imperialism*, New York: International Publishers, 1965, *Handbook of Revolutionary Warfare*, London: Panaf Publishers, 1968, and *Revolutionary Path*, New York: International Publishers, 1973).

The fate of Africa shall remain in the hands of foreigners as long as the continent remains divided and powerless.

The United States and Western Europe dominate the world today; in fact, West Europeans alone did so during the last 300 years or so when they were the imperial powers.

China is also on the rise as the next superpower after the United States. Even after the collapse of the Soviet Union which she built and dominated, Russia is still a world power in spite of her serious internal problems that threaten her very existence as a single political entity.

All these countries have one thing in common as world powers: Unity.

We Africans know that, just like everybody else does. No country has ever achieved power without unity. And no country has survived or developed without unity.

As Africans, we know what it means to be powerless in a world which respects nothing else, and is impressed by nothing less, except power. The question is why we are not united, knowing what it means to be powerless. As Julius Nyerere stated:

"Hardly a week passes but Africa is humiliated by outside powers. Our interests are ignored, our opinions are brushed aside, and our warnings disregarded. And this happens because the states of Africa are disunited – for no other reason than that.

Africa is ignored and exploited because we ourselves allow it to happen....

The power-hungry nations of the world, and the

exploiters of the world, must be laughing silently in watching us. For they see different states, which are tied together by the facts of geography and by mutual need, ignore their joint potential in the hopeless chase after the mirage of individual greatness. There is not one which could achieve it....

Africa will only be secure in its freedom, and only allow real economic prosperity for its people, when the present multitude of small states are replaced by one internationally sovereign authority."– (Julius Nyerere, *Freedom and Socialism: A Selection from Writings and Speeches 1965-1967*, Dar es Salaam, Tanzania: Oxford University Press, 1968, pp. 291, and 195. See also Nyerere, "A United States of Africa," in *The Journal of Modern African Studies,* Vol. 1, No. 1, March 1963).

The weakness of the modern African state is a constant and shameful reminder of the tragedy that befell Africa more than 100 years ago.

It was Africa's weakness and lack of unity which enabled Europeans to conquer us.

It led to our subjugation by a mere handful of them conquering vast expanses of territory inhabited by millions of people.

More than one hundred years after we were conquered and colonised, and at least six decades after we won independence ending colonial rule, it is the same weakness and lack of unity which is responsible for the plight and misery hundreds of millions of our people across the continent face everyday. And tragically, that is what distinguishes us – more than anybody else – from other people round the globe, earning us an unenviable distinction as the most depressed part of humanity. And statistics tell a tragic story.

It is our continent which has the largest number of the poorest countries in the world. It is also in Africa where you find the largest number of the weakest countries on

Earth.

There is no question that the modern African state has failed to live up to its expectations.

Its very existence in its present form has become a liability because of its irrelevance and weakness.

It is irrelevant because it operates as an alien institution not responsive to the needs of the people; a colonial legacy most African leaders have done nothing about since independence, as long as the institutions of power they inherited from the colonialists continue to benefit them.

It was more than just a desire for power which made them retain those institutions. Retention of the colonial power structure also amounted to submission at the psychological level to the might of Europe in all its manifestations. For, although our leaders fought for independence, many of them – by no means all – succumbed to indoctrination by the colonial rulers who taught them and the rest of us that everything European, including the oppressive colonial institutions they bequeathed to us upon attainment of independence, was superior to anything African.

We were therefore defeated not only on the battlefield but also in the realm of ideas. And in many cases, our conquerors became our heroes instead of our villains. Probably more than anything else, Europe conquered the mind of Africa, with many Africans falling prostrate at her feet in abject submission, glorifying her.

European armies did not invade Africa. Expeditionary forces were dispatched now and then on punitive missions against recalcitrant rulers, mainly chiefs, and their followers. But no major invasions were routinely launched except in a few cases: for example, by the British against the Ashanti in the Gold Coast and against the Kikuyu during Mau Mau in Kenya; and by the Germans against a coalition of several tribes during the Maji Maji uprising in Tanganyika: no fewer than 10 tribes, all in the southern half of the country, took part in the uprising – Ngoni,

Bunga, Mwera, Sagara, Zaramo, Matumbi, Kichi, Ikemba, Bena, and Pogoro.

But such major uprisings were not only few by comparison but also unsuccessful in many cases. And because of the limited number of military operations Europeans were able to carry out, it was through propagation of ideas, not through the barrel of the gun, that Europe won. Ideas are not spread by bullets.

It was the most successful psychological warfare ever waged against Africans by foreigners.

However, even in the few major wars launched by our conquerors, Africans fought back valiantly. Europeans were not the invincible force they thought they were or portrayed themselves to be.

They were sorely tested in Ethiopia, a country which was never colonised in spite of determined attempts by the Italians to subjugate it.

The British, in spite of their superior weapons, suffered a humiliating defeat at the hands of the Zulu.

Ashanti resistance to British rule in the Gold Coast fuelled nationalism.

In South West Africa, what is Namibia today, Africans resisted European penetration for 400 years from the 1400s to the 1800s.

Mau Mau ended British rule in Kenya. The freedom fighters sent the British packing. With typical imperialist arrogance, the colonial settlers called Kenya – "White Man's Country." Mau Mau proved that to be a historical fiction.

About 60 years earlier in neighbouring Tanganyika, the Hehe defeated the Germans.

Therefore, besides the fact that Africans in the end succumbed to imperial might, and many of them had indeed been brainwashed into believing that white is might is right, they at the same time exploded the myth that our invaders were invincible.

Still, Europe had demonstrated in no uncertain terms

that she was stronger than Africa. But wherein lay her strength?

Europe gave concrete expression to the idea of nationalism at home and abroad where European nationalism evolved into imperialism as the highest expression of national power.

When we talk about nationalism, we are talking about the collective attitude of a people toward their common destiny and their loyalty to the group to which they belong even if they don't have a common culture and a common language or even a territory; although more often than not, nationalism is identified with all those attributes collectively.

But it doesn't have to. For example, African countries are composed of different tribes or ethnic groups, each with its own history, language and culture. Yet they collectively constitute a single nation. Nigeria with more than 250 ethnic groups, the Democratic Republic of Congo (Congo-Kinshasa) with more than 200, and Tanzania with about 130, are some examples of great ethnic diversity transcended by national loyalties.

And in terms of territorial ownership as a legitimate criterion for nationhood, we see that it is not valid in all cases.

Before the establishment of Israel, Jews constituted a nation in the diaspora for 2,000 years without land, just as the Palestinians today constitute a nation although they don't have an independent state on a territory they call their homeland but don't control – it is controlled by Israel virtually as a colonial power.

In Africa, nationalism is given its highest expression on a continental scale as Pan-Africanism.

Unfortunately for us, there was no such continental phenomenon uniting us against our European invaders when they first set foot on our soil.

Even in the areas we call countries today, we didn't even know about each other except neighbouring tribes some of which were at each other's throat.

In most cases, the African nation then was the tribe; too small a unit on its own to successfully resist European invasion which became even more deadly because of the superior firepower of our invaders.

However, in spite of such narrow nationalism aptly described as tribalism, Africans were still able to build empires and kingdoms before the coming of Europeans. In fact, some of them were multinational states transcending ethnic boundaries and differences. They incorporated several different tribes into a single polity usually through conquest. Some of these empires and kingdoms lasted for centuries. That was African nationalism at its best.

This militant collective sentiment, nationalism is nothing but that, also served our conquerors well.

It was nationalism which Europeans used to mobilise forces on their behalf in the clash of civilisations between Africa and Europe.

Nationalism, more than anything else, propelled Europeans to the top. It was nationalist zeal, combined with greed, which inspired them to embark on foreign missions of territorial conquest, leading them to hoist the imperial flag in the name of the motherland or fatherland in different parts of the world.

It was also nationalism which inspired them to push the frontiers of knowledge in order to fight poverty, ignorance and disease, and finally attempt to conquer space.

You will not find a single European country which does not boast of eminent men and women in science and other disciplines. Among them are those who have earned distinction as towering figures in their fields on a global scale. By contrast, Africa's record is dismal.

Conquered, oppressed and exploited, and stripped of our dignity, we became mere tools in the hands of our conquerors.

And in spite of all the damage they caused us, there

were many Africans who tried desperately to become more European than the Europeans themselves, as our conquerors laughed at us for aping them so slavishly.

Is there anything humanly possible Europeans did we Africans could not have done, on our own, and probably even better? As Frantz Fanon reminds us in *The Wretched of the Earth*:

"So, comrades, let us not pay tribute to Europe by creating states, institutions, and societies which draw their inspiration from her. Humanity is waiting for something other from us than such an imitation, which would be almost an obscene caricature.

If we want to turn Africa into a new Europe, then let us leave the destiny of our countries to Europeans. They will know how to do it better than the most gifted among us. But if we want humanity to advance a step further, if we want to bring it up to a different level than that which Europe has shown it, then we must invent and we must make discoveries.

If we wish to live up to our people's expectations, we must seek the response elsewhere than in Europe. For Europe, for ourselves and for humanity, comrades, we must turn over a new leaf, we must work out new concepts, and try to set afoot a new man." – (Frantz Fanon, *The Wretched of the Earth*, New York: Grove Press, 1963, p. 239).

Unfortunately, even today, many Africans are still doing everything they can to be what Europe is – and that includes America, her offshoot – and do everything Europe has done including repeating her mistakes, which they don't see as mistakes.

That is because they want to de-Africanise themselves and be anything else but what they are.

We are not saying we can't or shouldn't learn from other people – we can and we should if we have to.

The question is: Why do we want to be carbon copies and a replica of everything non-African?

Why don't we, especially those among us who want to copy others so much, have anything to offer, something positive and original non-Africans can learn from us?

Even our schools and other institutions remain a replica of Europe.

This slavish imitation not only stunts our intellectual growth but *defiles* the African personality.

It is true that we fought to free ourselves from our conquerors. And it was a noble struggle, not only to regain our land and independence but also our dignity. As Patrice Lumumba said on 30 June 1960, the day Congo won independence from Belgium:

"We have known ironies, insults and blows which we had to undergo morning, noon, and night because we were Negroes. We have seen our lands spoiled in the name of laws which differed according to whether they dealt with a black man or a white...

Of this struggle, one of tears, fire and blood, we are proud to the very depths of our being, for it was a noble and just struggle, absolutely necessary in order to bring to an end the humiliating slavery which had been imposed upon us by force...

We shall show the whole world what the black man can do when he is allowed to work in freedom and we shall make of the Congo a shining example for the whole of Africa." – (Patrice Lumumba, quoted in Rolf Italiaander, *The New Leaders of Africa*, Englewood Cliffs, New Jersey, USA: Prentice Hall, 1961, p. 159; K. R. Minogue, *Nationalism*, Baltimore, Maryland, USA: Penguin Books, 1970, p. 32; Catherine Hoskyns, *The Congo Since Independence: January 1960 – December 1961*, Oxford: Oxford University Press, 1965, pp. 85 – 86; John Reader, *Africa: A Biography of the Continent*, New York: Alfred A. Knopf, 1998, p. 657. See also Lumumba in Hans Kohn and Wallace Sokolsky, *African Nationalism in the Twentieth Century*, Princeton, New Jersey: D. Van Nostrand Company, Inc., 1965; Lumumba, "The Independence of the Congo," in James Duffy and Robert A. Manners, eds., *Africa Speaks*, Princeton, New Jersey: D. Van Nostrand Company, Inc., 1961).

It was a sentiment shared across the continent. As one Nigerian political party, the Action Group led by Chief Obafemi Awolowo, stated in 1960 in its policy paper on a proposed West African Union, consummation of such a union would prove to the world that:

"Negro States, though the last to come, are the first to use their brains for the conquest of the forces that have kept men apart." – (Action Group, "Policy Paper on the West African Union…and on the Scientific and Cultural Development of Nigeria," Lagos, Nigeria, 1960, pp. 6, and 1-2; cited by Ali A. Mazrui, *Towards A Pax Africana*, London: Weidenfeld & Nicolson, 1968, pp. 86, and 87).

It went on to state that attainment of independence by Nigeria and other African countries was not an end in itself but a means towards ends which included winning respect for all the people of African descent in the diaspora "by the creation of the Negro world…We must ensure that we make a distinct and worthwhile contribution to the civilization of the world." – (Ibid.).

And it is a noble goal, especially after being so humiliated by our imperial masters.

Yet there are many among us who continue to thunder praise for our conquerors and refuse to think for themselves.

It is true that the rest of mankind have also been conquered at one time or another. But a significant number of them never stopped to think for themselves as much as we Africans have. We go to other countries to learn almost everything – including our own history taught to us by foreigners at their institutions of higher learning which departments of African history – more than foreigners come to learn from us, if at all.

Many other cultures which were conquered, or which collapsed from within without any externally engineered forces impinging on them, continued to build on their past and even pushed frontiers of knowledge. We could have done the same thing.

Instead we, especially our leaders and the elite, have repudiated our past on which we could have built a solid foundation for our societies without necessarily insulating ourselves from everything modern. That is because we have been busy trying to be like Europe, America, and everything else but what we are.

We have lost our minds.

The stubborn belief among untold numbers of non-blacks that black people are indeed less intelligent than everybody else continues to haunt us because it is an enduring legacy of the imperial conquest of Africa by the West which was "justified" on genetic grounds.

If our conquerors admitted that we were equal to them, then their conquest of Africa and the entire imperial edifice would have had no rationale for its existence on our continent.

It is a legacy that will continue to dog us probably until the end of time; thanks to Western imperialism founded on the doctrine of white supremacy which reached its apogee in apartheid South Africa, a country which is now probably scarred for life even after the abolition of that abominable institution.

But as we take stock of our past and present, assessing the damage inflicted on us by the West while at the same time acknowledging the benefits of Western civilisation brought to us, although these were only peripheral to the central mission of imperial conquest and in fact facilitated this diabolical mission; and as we assess and acknowledge our successes and failures, past and present, in different fields of human endeavour, we must never fail to pay tribute to our ancestors who – before the coming of Europeans – laid the foundation upon which we can build a prosperous future.

It is a lasting achievement they bequeathed us without which we would not be where we are today. As Kwame Nkrumah stated in his speech on the motion for Ghana's independence he delivered before the Gold Coast Legislative Assembly on 10 July 1953:

"In the very early days of the Christian era, long before England had assumed any importance, long even before her people had united into a nation, our ancestors had attained a great empire, which lasted until the eleventh century, when it fell before the attacks of the Moors of the North.

At its height, that empire stretched from Timbuktu to Bamako, and even as far as to the Atlantic. It is said that lawyers and scholars were much respected in that empire, and that the inhabitants of Ghana wore garments of wool, cotton, silk and velvet. There was trade in copper, gold and textile fabrics, and jewels and weapons of gold and silver were carried.

Thus may we take pride in the name of Ghana, not out of romanticism, but as an inspiration for the future.

It is right and proper that we should know about our past. For just as the future moves from the present so the present has emerged from the past. Nor need we be ashamed of our past. There was much in it of glory.

What our ancestors achieved in the context of their contemporary society, gives us confidence that we can create, out of that past, a glorious future..." – (Kwame Nkrumah, Kwame Nkrumah's "Speech on the Motion for Independence" to the Gold Coast Legislative Assembly, Accra, Gold Coast, 10 July 1953; reprinted in George

Padmore, *Pan-Africanism or Communism?: The Coming Struggle for Africa*, London: Dennis Dobson, 1956, Appendix III, p. 406).

But in the history of nationalism, glories of the past are not enough without a history of military exploits or some kind of heroic resistance against foreign invaders or other enemies. And we have no shortage of that.

Africans resisted in all parts of the continent. We already know about the Ashanti, the Xhosa, the Zulu, the Hehe, the Kikuyu, as we learned earlier. There were many others.

Samori Ture, master of guerrilla warfare and great-grandfather of the late President Sekou Toure of Guinea (1922 – 1984), successfully led his forces against the French in several encounters in an area that became Guinea and beyond its borders. He had a well-disciplined army and established the Mandinka empire, also known as the Wassoulou empire, and seriously threatened French expansionist ambitions during the 1880s and 1890s in that part of the continent.

He not only resisted French occupation but continued to wage guerrilla warfare against the French long after his empire had been conquered.

The Fulani in Northern Nigeria waged religious wars against the British in confrontations which were as religious as they were nationalistic.

In French Cameroon, the Adamawa emirates fiercely resisted French rule and occupation.

In East Africa, in addition to the wars by the Hehe and the Maji Maji uprising against the Germans in Tanganyika, and the Mau Mau war by the Kikuyu against the British in Kenya, other people in the region also put up stiff resistance against the European invaders.

In Somalia, the Somalis waged an intense religious-nationalist war against the British from 1891 to 1920.

In Ethiopia, the Italians suffered a crushing defeat at

Adowa in 1896. And a generation later, the Ethiopians strongly resisted the Italian invasion in 1935 – 36.

In Uganda, the Baganda waged war against the British, as did the Nandii, the Kipsigis, and the Giriama in neighbouring Kenya long before Mau Mau.

Further south in Rhodesia, the Ndebele and the Shona fought the British settlers and other whites from South Africa during the 1880s and 1890s.

When our ancestors lost some of the wars, it was not necessarily because they did not try hard enough. They fought hard against our European invaders. As Fanon put it in an appropriate historical context:

"Each generation must out of relative obscurity discover its mission, fulfil it, or betray it.

We must rid ourselves of the habit, now that we are in the thick of the fight, of minimizing the actions of our forefathers or of feigning incomprehension when considering their silence and passivity.

They fought as well as they could, with the arms they possessed then; and if the echoes of their struggle have not resounded in the international arena, we must realize that the reason for their silence lies less in their lack of heroism than in the fundamentally different international situation of our time." – (Fanon, *Wretched of the Earth,* op. cit., pp. 206 – 207).

In Sierra Leone, the indigenous people rose up against the British in 1898. Led by Bai Bureh, they were members of the Temne and Loko ethnic groups in northern Sierra Leone in an insurrection that was nationalist in inspiration.

Bai Bureh did not recognise British rule. He wanted the colonial rulers to go back where they came from and leave Sierra Leoneans alone to manage their own affairs. He declared war on them.

Fighters from other ethnic groups, besides the Temne and the Loko, also joined his army of freedom fighters.

They included the Limba, the Kissi and the Kuranko or Koranko, also of northern Sierra Leone.

The uprising he led symbolised resistance to alien rule and was relevant to other ethnic ethnic groups in Sierra Leone not just to those in the north in their quest for self-determination.

In Angola, the Bakongo and the Ovimbundu rose up against the Portuguese in 1913, centuries after their colonial masters founded the colony in the 1500s; an uprising which was a continuation of the struggle that had been going on for centuries by members of other ethnic groups as well.

The next major uprising was in 1961 by the MPLA (Popular Movement for the Liberation of Angola) which finally led to independence 14 years later in 1975.

There was resistance, including armed resistance, even in some areas where Europeans least expected to encounter such opposition to their imperial adventures.

Not only was such resistance a continental phenomenon; it lasted for years, and even for decades, in different parts of Africa and was transformed into political opposition leading to the formation of nationalist movements which finally led to independence.

It is this kind of nationalist resistance which prompted Nkrumah, who blazed the trail for the African independence movement, to state in the Gold Coast Legislative Assembly in his speech on the motion for Ghana's independence:

"In calling up our past, it is meet, on a historic occasion such as this, to pay tribute to those ancestors of ours who laid our national traditions, and those others who opened the path which made it possible to reach today the great moment at which we stand.

As with our enslaved brothers dragged from these shores to the United States and to the West Indies, throughout our tortuous history, we have not been docile under the heel of the conqueror…We constantly formed ourselves into cohesive blocs as a means of resistance against the alien force within our borders.

And so today we recall the birth of the Ashanti nation through Okomfo Anokye and Nana Osei Tutu and the symbolism entrenched in the Golden Stool (Hear! Hear! Hear!); the valiant wars against the British, the banishment of Nana Prempah the First to the Seychelles Islands; the temporary disintegration of the nation and its subsequent reunification…

Then the Fanti Confederation. The earliest manifestation of Gold Coast nationalism occurred in 1868 when Fanti Chiefs attempted to form the Fanti Confederation in order to defend themselves against the might of Ashanti and the incipient encroachment of British merchants. It was also a union of the coastal states for mutual economic and social development. This was declared a dangerous conspiracy with the consequent arrest of its leaders.

Then the Aborigines Right Protection Society was the next nationalist movement to be formed with its excellent aims and objects, and by putting up their titanic fight for which we cannot be sufficiently grateful, formed an unforgettable bastion for the defence of our God-given land and thus preserved our inherent right to freedom. Such men as Mensah-Sarbah, Atto-Ahuma, Sey and Wood have played their role in this great fight. (Hear! Hear!)….

Were not our ancestors ruling themselves before the white man came to our shores?….

To assert that certain people are capable of ruling themselves while others are not yet 'ready,' as the saying goes, smacks to me more of imperialism than reason." – (Nkrumah, "Speech on Motion for Independence," *Pan-Africanism or Communism?: The Coming Struggle for Africa*, op. cit., pp. 406-07, and 409).

Like any other people, we take pride in what our

ancestors did to resist foreign invasion.

But besides the history of nationalist resistance, there is another aspect of national honour people take pride in. And that is simplicity as a virtue. Thus, a poor African peasant living in abject poverty in the hinterland of Africa is not in any way inferior to the financial barons on Wall Street who are the pinnacle of plutocratic arrogance.

It is true that in terms of material things, he has nothing compared to them and to other people in industrialised countries including the poorest such as Portugal, one of Africa's former colonial powers. But he may possess something intangible even the rich and famous and members of Western civilisation may not have. That is simplicity.

It is a national virtue. For example, German nationalist philosopher Johann Fichte talks about German "simplicity and credulity," implying that his fellow countrymen are virtuous, since simplicity and credulity can mean virtue depending on the context in which those two attributes are articulated. And being the fanatical patriot he is, he also talks about Germans as a people who speak "a language which is shaped to express the truth." – (Johann Fichte, quoted by H. S. Reiss, *The Political Thought of the German Romantics 1793 – 1815*, Oxford: Oxford University Press, 1955, p. 105. See also F. Barnard, *Herder's Social and Political Thought* (Oxford University Press, 1965).

Railing against Gallic cosmopolitanism which he detests just like any other foreign influence, a point he forcefully makes in his fervently nationalistic works *The Closed Commercial State,* and *Addresses to the German Nation* he delivered as lectures at the University of Berlin in 1807-08, Fichte goes on to state that "foreign cunning easily outmatched German simplicity and credulity." – (Fichte, Ibid.).

That is the same fate that also befell Africa at the hands of our cunning imperial masters, including Fichte's own fatherland Germany which – in spite of "German simplicity and credulity" – was one of the imperial powers that invaded our continent in pursuit of material gain, national prestige and other national interests. Morality was the last thing on the minds of our invaders as far as our interests were concerned. We did not even exist.

Thus, besides material civilisation – for which the West is best known probably more than anybody else and which needs to be tempered or counterbalanced with compassion, generosity and other virtues – there is also moral civilisation.

It is a civilisation whose height is not measured by how high rockets shoot into the sky or how deep submarines plumb the depths of oceans, or how far man has gone in exploring the mysteries of life, but by how man values another man. As Nkrumah stated on that fateful day, 10 July 1953 when he formally demanded Ghana's independence in his address to the Gold Coast Legislative Assembly:

"In our daily lives, we may lack those material comforts regarded as essential by the standards of the modern world; but we have the gifts of laughter and joy, a love of music, a lack of malice, an absence of the desire for vengeance for our wrongs, all things of intrinsic worth in a world sick of injustice, revenge, fear and want." – (Nkrumah, "Speech on Motion for Independence," op. cit., p. 412).

It is a simplicity – as a virtue – which neither glorifies things material nor denigrates things spiritual; neither justifies poverty nor condones greed. It is a virtue rooted in our past, a heritage we can harness to build a modern African society without compromising its essence embodied in our traditional values.

It is a heritage Europe tried to destroy when she invaded Africa. And that is only one of the saddest chapters in the turbulent history of relations between Africa and the West through the centuries. As Nkrumah stated less than four years before he led Ghana to become the first black African country to win independence:

"We feel that there is much the world can learn from those of us who belong to what we might term the pre-technological societies. These are values which we must not sacrifice unheedingly in pursuit of material progress....

We have to work hard to evolve new patterns, new social customs, new attitudes to life, so that while we seek the material, cultural and economic advancement of our country, while we raise their standards of life, we shall not sacrifice their fundamental happiness. That…has been the greatest tragedy of Western society since the Industrial Revolution." – (Ibid.).

It is also a tragedy that Africa still suffers and which she has suffered since the advent of colonial rule.

Despite the quantum leaps she has made in terms of material civilisation, sometimes to her detriment as well as ours, the West has not produced the best in many other areas. And some of her biggest victims have been black people, not only in Africa, but in the Western world itself. It is a fate that has befallen the children of Africa virtually round the globe in terms of treatment by other people. We are universally despised simply because of what we are: black people. As Professor Harold Cruse, a black American, stated in his book *Rebellion or Revolution?*:

"The American Negro must stand up and fight his way out of the social trap in which Western civilization has ensnared him…Western civilization is intellectually, spiritually and morally bankrupt.

It is a civilization that is no longer able to originate

creative ideas in social thinking – and America is no exception to this creative decline that is sapping the vitality of the Western world...

The racial crisis in America is more than a question of what white Americans are going to do about their subclass of exploited Negro wards. It is also a broader question: which way is America going, up or down?

Beyond that, it is a question of which way is white civilization going?

How do white people, Americans included, propose to accommodate themselves to an emerging world of non-white peoples over whom whites no longer have the right of unilateral dispensation?

The racial crisis in America is an internal reflection of this contemporary world-wide problem of readjustment between ex-colonial masters and ex-colonial subjects.

The so-called 'democratic heritage' of the American tradition has served as historical camouflage to hide the fact that America participated in colonialism through its peculiar institution of slavery.

Although a very special kind of colonialism, slavery was an organic offshoot of European subjugation of Africa and the New World.

After the Civil War, the Negro was transformed into a semi-colonial people no different from any other semi-colonial people in South Africa or parts of Latin America."
– Harold Cruse, *Rebellion or Revolution?*, New York: William Morrow & Co., 1968, pp. 104-05).

German historian and philosopher Oswald Spengler (1880 – 1936) also addressed the same subject about the fall of Western civilisation. He expressed his cyclic view of history in *The Decline of the West*, 1918 – 1922, a study of the rise and fall of civilisations.

He believed that Western civilisation was entering a period of decline, a view much favoured between World War I and World War II.

The Decline of the West, which was his major work, was published in two volumes and brought him worldwide fame. The first one was published in 1918.

He contended that every culture passes through a life cycle from youth to maturity and old age to death. Western culture, he believed, had proceeded through this same cycle and had entered the period of decline from which there was no escape.

Spengler upheld the ideal of obedience to the state and supported German hegemony in Europe. But his refusal to support Nazi theories of racial superiority led to his ostracism after the Nazis came to power in 1933.

Although Professor Harold Cruse tackles the same subject Spengler did about the decline of the West, he does so from a different perspective as a black nationalist and in relation to the destiny of black people in the American context; an analysis that is nevertheless, by linkage, relevant to Africa since the continent is also the homeland of black Americans and was once subjugated by the West including the United States herself through outright enslavement of Africans who were taken there in chains to work as slaves.

And she still exercises control over Africa in many ways even today, including the exploitation of the continent's resources by multinational corporations in this era of globalisation dominated by the West. The biggest multinationals exploiting Africa are American or controlled by the United States. As Cruse states with black nationalist passion:

"(Black people should not be) overawed by the glitter and glamor of a steel-riveted and chrome-plated Western world in the last stages of cultural and spiritual decline...

For any Negro to get, with childlike and empty-minded mimicry, to have the Negro image further distorted by its inclusion in the whitefaced orgy of spiritual decadence is to ask that the Negro participate with whites in their senseless and insane debasement of every humanistic social value that ever came out of the Western cultural tradition…

The Negro is bent on integrating into nothing…It is the same thing as asking to join the dead and the dying at the gates of the graveyard of dead civilizations for any Negro to seek integration in American culture." – (H. Cruse, *Rebellion or Revolution?, ibid.,* pp. 123, and 122).

It is a language typical of nationalist thinking. And one should expect it from oppressed people like blacks. The sentiment expressed by Cruse is also shared by many Africans on the African continent itself, not just by American blacks like him. As Professor Ali Mazrui, a Kenyan and one of the most internationally renowned African scholars, states in his book *The Africans*:

"The West has contributed far less to the industrialization of Africa than Africa has contributed to the industrial civilization of the West....

The materialism of Western civilization, the superiority of Western science and technology at their home base in the West, and the glitter and temptations of Western life-styles, have all combined to pose a significant threat especially to the younger generations....

As these Western institutions grind to a standstill in Africa, causing new areas of poverty and deprivation, the glitter of Western civilization begins to dim." – (Ali A. Mazrui, *The Africans*, London: BBC Publications, 1986, quoted by George B. N. Ayittey, *Africa Betrayed*, New York: St. Martin's Press, 1992, p. 29).

There is ample evidence of that across the African continent, especially in the cities which have sustained the biggest blow from the negative impact of Western civilisation.

Even the rapid spread of AIDS can partly be attributed

to Western decadence in African cities.

President Museveni said Ugandans traditionally shunned extramarital sex, and one tribe used to pull out the eyes of anyone who had sex before marriage.

The AIDS epidemic across Africa has been attributed to the decadence of Western values brought into the continent by Europeans, although this is a highly controversial thesis and not defensible in all contexts. But it has nationalist appeal, nonetheless, and has been forcefully articulated by President Yoweri Museveni of Uganda in spite of its obvious flaws.

People in Africa have been involved in extra-marital relations and sex before marriage and long before the coming of Europeans. We are not a paragon of virtue anymore than any other people are.

Yet, there is no question that promotion of sex by the West – in the media including television – has played a major role in encouraging promiscuity, especially among the youth across Africa and in other parts of the Third World, justified on the grounds that it is an integral part of the glamour and glitter of Western life styles the rest of the world needs to emulate.

In a speech in Uganda's capital Kampala on 21 September 1998 at a conference for AIDS victims, President Museveni said the AIDS virus spread rapidly through Africa because Africans began imitating the promiscuity of Westerners.

There is ample evidence of that after Africans were exposed to full radiation of Western civilisation and predatory capitalism especially in the urban areas; a pernicious influence which shows there is an imperative need for Africa to insulate herself from such negative exposure.

President went on to say:

"This sexual laxity today is a colonial phenomenon. We have lost the traditional values, and yet we do not have a sophisticated health network of the modern world." – (Yoweri Museveni, quoted in "Uganda Leader Links Western Values to AIDS in Africa," in *The Boston Globe,* September 22, 1998, p. A-8).

There is no question that the invasion of Africa by Europeans wreaked havoc across the spectrum, cultural and spiritual, as well as material. As Professor Mazrui states:

"The West harmed Africa's indigenous technological development in a number of ways...(because of the) shallowness of Western institutions, the lopsided nature of colonial acculturation, (and) the moral contradictions of Western political tutelage....
(Even) the political decay is partly a consequence of colonial institutions without cultural roots in Africa....
The pervasive atmosphere in much of the land is one of rust and dust, stagnation and decay, especially within those institutions which were originally bequeathed by the West...(signalling) the slow death of an alien civilization... (and Africa's revulsion) against westernization masquerading as modernity." – (A. Mazrui, *The Africans,* op. cit., pp. 164, 199, 210, 204, and 211; George B. N. Ayittey, *Africa In Chaos*, New York: St. Martin's Press, 1998, p. 38. See also Thomas Pakenham, *The Scramble for Africa: The White Man's Conquest of the Dark Continent from 1876 to 1912*, New York: Random House, 1991).

Articulating the same position taken by Frantz Fanon in *The Wretched of the Earth* and *A Dying Colonialism* and in his other writings, the same position taken by other African writers and analysts such as Ngugi wa Thiong'o, Mazrui says the world has nothing to lose if Western civilization collapses. As he stated in *The Washington Times,* 13 November 1990:

"The decline of Western civilization might well be at hand. It is in the interest of humanity that such a decline should take place." – (A. Mazrui, quoted in *The Washington Times,* November 13, 1990, p. G-4; G. Ayittey, "Africa Betrayed," op. cit., p. 29. See also Fanon, *Wretched of the Earth, A Dying Colonialism,* and *Toward the African Revolution,* op. cit.).

What we have here is a blunt appraisal and assessment of technological and material civilisation of which the West is its apogee.

From Nkrumah's assessment to Fanon's and Museveni's; from Mazrui's to Cruse's and that of others in the African world, and even from the judgment of some members of the Western world itself such as German historian and philosopher Oswald Spengler, the conclusion is obvious: Material civilisation may have reached its zenith in the West.

It is also the *bane* of civilisation itself.

It is in the West where spiritual awareness is at its nadir. Materialism has corrupted the soul of the West.

It was also materialism which propelled the West into Africa, without invitation, to exploit her resources and enslave her people, one of the most tragic chapters in the history of mankind. As W.E. B. Du Bois stated in his book *Darkwater*: *Voices from Within the Veil*:

"The indictment of Africa against Europe is grave. For four hundred years white Europe was the chief support of that trade in human beings which first and last robbed Africa of a hundred million human beings, transformed the face of her social life, overthrew organized government, distorted ancient industry, and snuffed out the lights of cultural development.

Today instead of removing laborers from Africa to distant slavery, industry built on a new slavery approaches

Africa to deprive the natives of their land, to force them to toil, and to reap all the profit for the white world." – (W.E.B. Du Bois, *Darkwater, Voices from Within the Veil*, New York: Schocken Books, 1969, pp. 57 – 58).

Without Africa, the West would not have the industrial might she has today. And without the minerals and other resources she continues to get from Africa, Western civilisation as we know it would collapse overnight.

But it was the exploitation of Africa by Europe in earlier years, including the enslavement of millions of Africans, which laid the foundation of Western industrial progress. As George Bernard Shaw stated in one of his essays, which was also hailed as a great literary achievement, "Transition to Social Democracy":

"The relationship of a negro to the human race was far more distant than that of a gorilla is now admitted to be. Thus, when the discovery of the New World began that economic revolution which changed every manufacturing town into a mere booth in the world's fair, and quite altered the immediate objects and views of producers, English adventurers took to the sea in a frame of mind peculiarly favorable to commercial success. They were unaffectedly pious, and had the force of character which is only possible to men who are founded on convictions.

At the same time, they regarded piracy as a brave and patriotic pursuit, and the slave trade as a perfectly honest branch of commerce, adventurous enough to be consistent with the honor of a gentleman, and lucrative enough to make it well worth the risk. When they stole the cargo of a foreign ship, or made a heavy profit on a batch of slaves, they regarded their success as a direct proof of divine protection.

The owners of accumulated wealth hastened to 'venture' their capital with these men. Persons of all the richer degrees, from Queen Elizabeth downward, took shares in the voyages of the merchant adventurers. The returns justified their boldness; and the foundation of the industrial greatness and the industrial shame of the eighteenth and nineteenth centuries was laid: modern Capitalism thus arising in enterprises for which men are now, by civilized nations, hung or shot as human vermin. And it is curious to see still, in the commercial adventures of our own time, the same incongruous combination of piety and rectitude with the most unscrupulous and revolting villainy."– (George Bernard Shaw, "Transition to Social Democracy," in *Fabian Essays*, London: George Allen and Unwin Ltd., 1889; reprinted in Marshall Goldman, ed., *Comparative Economic Systems: A Reader*, New York: Random House, 1971, p. 204).

And because of the pervasive nature of Western influence, the negative impact of this onslaught has reached all parts of the world, including Africa where the devastation wrought is difficult to contain because of our inability to resist such penetration; our weakness attributed to various causes including weak moral foundations among some of the victims; weak social structures, endemic poverty and lack of awareness of the diabolical nature of many aspects of Westernisation or Western influence.

One of those aspects inextricably linked with Westernisation is the colonisation and exploitation of Africa which has left African countries powerless to cope with a multitude of problems including the spread of disease.

That is mainly because of economic underdevelopment which is the direct result of imperial rule that resulted in the subjugation and exploitation of Africans and left them at the mercy of the colonial powers including others such as the United States which continue to exploit Africans just as much and are virtually the new colonial rulers – together with the former colonial powers who really never left.

The presence of all those powers in Africa, and the influence they continue to spread and exerscise, has had a devastating impact on the wellbeing of Africans and the continent's destiny.

As I stated earlier, the sheer scope of such influence and its attraction especially among the youth who are mesmerised by the glitter of the West is far beyond our capacity to contain let alone neutralise it. That is especially the case in urban centres whose irresistible magnetic power continues to attract millions of people in search of better life which is synonymous with Westernisation.

Africa can continue along this path only at her own peril.

Chapter Five:

Conquest of the mind:
Our experience and destiny
as Africans

MY LIFE under British colonial rule in my home country, what was then Tanganyika before it united with Zanzibar to form Tanzania, was not a unique experience. It was only a part of the cumulative experience we Africans had to endure under imperial subjugation.

I was born a colonial subject like millions of other Tanganyikans. Therefore, the story of my life is, in general and in some fundamental respects, a microcosm of the experience of other Tanganyikans who were also born during the colonial period.

It is the story of other Tanganyikans not only in terms of colonial domination but also in terms of racial injustices perpetrated against them.

Racial injustices had the biggest impact on the lives of black people – far more than they did on the lives of other non-white Tanganyikans. And that was for one simple reason. Black people constituted the vast majority of the population. They were also at the bottom of the social hierarchy in a society structured like a pyramid, with whites on top.

But it is also a story of racial accommodation in which

racial minorities had plenty of room to continue living their lives without fear of the black majority who were to assume power after the end of colonial rule. It is also a story of racial harmony in a country where members of different races got along well even if they were socially distant from each other, as was indeed the case.

But my life under colonial rule is also my story, very personal in many respects, in spite of its wider relevance as an individual's experience reflective of what other Tanganyikans also experienced as colonial subjects, each of them also with a personal story to tell about that experience.

Growing up in the 1950s, I experienced a form of apartheid and racial segregation my fellow countrymen and women also experienced even if I did not fully understand it, the way adults did, because of my age. I spent my first twelve years under British colonial rule in a decade when agitation for independence was at its peak, finally leading to independence for Tanganyika, the first country in East Africa to emerge from colonial rule.

Yet my story and the individual stories of other Tanganyikans – Africans in general across the continent – is one story set in the broader context not only of the imperial conquest of Africa but also of its impact on our wellbeing and destiny as a people. We are still an integral part of the Western world in terms of influence and domination.

Our dignity has been wounded and identity imperiled by constant bombardment from the cultural forces unleashed by Western civilisation with the full backing of its imperial might even in the cultural arena in a world where Western influence is becoming increasingly dominant in this era of globalisation and has, in fact, been that way even before then. It seems to have conquered other cultures in many areas even if in limited ways.

That has been our fate since colonisation. It includes the policy of assimilation – although it never really worked for the vast majority of the people, especially the masses – in the French and Portuguese colonies which was one of the most brazen and worst attempts to de-Africanise Africans.

All that has put conscious Africans – those who are aware of and care about our vulnerable position in these culture wars – to be on the defensive by respecting and protecting our cultures and values and by taking an uncompromising stand against the propagation of alien ideas which pollute and pervert African minds and threaten our identity and integrity. There is no better way to undermine Africa.

Our identity, indeed our very being, is rooted in traditional Africa. Take that way, or ignore it, the African renaissance we talk so much about is impossible.

It is suicidal for us to help our conquerors denigrate traditional Africa in this "clash of civilisations" – to borrow Professor Samuel Huntington's phrase – whose foot solders on the side of our conquerors include Westernised Africans some of whom have been so brainwashed that they have ceased to be African in thought and spirit.

Conquest does not give conquerors the moral authority to denigrate and rule others; nor does it give them the right to think for them and to shape their destiny. It only gives them the immoral authority to abuse them; hardly grounds for claims of moral superiority by conquerors over their victims.

The "right" to abuse is derived from the power conquerors have to subjugate others. Such power has no moral constraints on it, not even from the morality of individuals who exercise it even if they rebel against authority and refuse to fulfill their obligations.

Only power has the power to restrain itself – which is not in its nature to do so. Its only antidote is counterpower if it is enough to defeat or extract concessions from those in power. This has to come from organised resistance by the oppressed; which we did not have when our conquerors – European invaders – came until we mobilised forces of *unified* resistance later.

Ironically, we used the same institutions they brought to rule us – constitutions, judiciaries, legislatures and so on – to press and articulate our demands but which only replaced our traditional institutions of authority, governance, representation and conflict resolution and were not superior to ours; only different in the way they – ours and theirs – operated but with the same purpose and objective of achieving social order and justice.

The traditional institutions of authority over ethnic groups – tribes – across our continent constituted states.

It is not true that Africa was stateless – did not have states – before the advent of colonial rule. They existed in different parts of the continent in varying degrees of organisation and success.

Some were more centralised than others. And there were those which were more decentralised, especially if they administered large territories inhabited by different ethnic groups which were united in a confederation or a highly decentralised form of federation such as the Fanti Confederation in what is now Ghana.

Some of the most centralised traditional states included Buganda, a kingdom which formed the nucleus of the modern nation of Uganda. Other traditional kingdoms – hence states – in Uganda included Bunyoro, Ankole, and the princedom of Busoga, although Buganda became the dominant kingdom.

In Ruanda-Urundi, what is now Rwanda and Burundi, the Tutsi established a centralised kingdom in which they became the dominant group over the Hutu majority. The kingdom was ruled by a *mwami* (king or queen).

There were similar kingdoms in the region including one ruled by a female, Mwami Theresa Ntare VI, queen of the kingdom of Heru in Buha, western Tanzania.

There was, in the same East African region, the

Karagwe kingdom in what is now Tanzania. It was located in an area that is now northwestern Tanzania bordering Rwanda.

There were other kingdoms in the Great Lakes region including the Kitara empire also known as Bunyoro-Kitara or the kingdom of Bakitara. It was a product of the fragmentation of the Chwezi empire which led to the emergence of a number of autonomous states in the region with strong traditional rulers and well-established governments.

There was also the Busongora kingdom located between what is now Rwanda and the kingdom of Bunyoro in what is now southwestern Uganda.

Further fragmentation of some of these states led to the emergence of strong chiefdoms, another form of institutionalised authority prevalent in many parts of Africa among various ethnic groups; testament to the fact that well-organised government and law and order was the norm rather than the exception even among smaller political and social entities formed by members of different "tribes" – ethnic groups.

In what is Ghana today and before it became the Gold Coast, there was the Ashanti kingdom. It was ruled by a king, the *asantehene*, and was one of the most powerful in Africa before the advent of colonial rule.

Determined to remain independent, the Ashanti fought the British in one of the bloodiest wars in the continent's colonial history.

There were other kingdoms and states in precolonial Gold Coast in the north, east and west, not just in the central region inhabited by the Ashanti. They included the Mamprusi kingdom covering northern and northeastern Ghana and parts of Burkina Faso; the Dagbon kingdom founded by the Dagomba people in what is now the Northern Region; the Gonja kingdom established by the Gonja also in the Northern Region; the Akuapem and Akropong states in what is now southeastern Ghana which later united and formed the Akropong-Akuapem kingdom; and the Denkyira kingdom which was the first and largest among the Akan people until it was conquered and replaced by the Ashanti kingdom.

Those are just some examples. There were other states and kingdoms in the precolonial period in the region which includes an area that became the Gold Coast.

There were also well-established states and kingdoms in what came to be the countries of Gabon – the kingdom of Orungu which was the most powerful in the area; Dahomey – the Fon kingdom whose founders, the Fon, were also the main founders of the kingdom of Dahomey; Chad – the Kanem-Bornu empire which also covered parts of northeastern Nigeria; Upper Volta (Burkina Faso) – Mossi kingdoms; Ivory Coast – the Kong empire and the states of Gyaman also known as Jamang and Baule; Guinea – it was a part of the Ghana, Mali and Songhai empires; Mali – Mali kingdom; Senegal – Jolof or Wolof empire.

The Hausa of Nigeria and other parts of West Africa also established a number of well-governed states which collectively constituted the Hausa kingdom, with Kano being the most powerful city state in the kingdom which existed as a confederation without a central government.

And there was Samori Ture discussed earlier. It was testament to his leadership qualities and military skills that he was able to establish a successful empire when the imperial powers were busy destroying traditional kingdoms and other powerful states which had been built in different parts of the continent before colonial rule.

He defeated the French in many battles including a heavily armed French army which used heavy artillery against his soldiers before he was finally captured and exiled to Gabon where he died in captivity.

There was also the Toucouleur empire in what is Mali today. It was a federation of chiefdoms, a form of union that was prevalent in many parts of the continent which did not have highly centralised states such as the Buganda kingdom and others.

There was also the Bamana empire in what became the country of Mali. It was formed after the collapse of the Mali empire and was a centralised state.

In what is Nigeria today, there were highly organised kingdoms among the Yoruba – the Oyo empire being one of the most powerful; it even dominated the kingdom of Dahomey in what is now Benin. The Yoruba were well-known for their city states long before Europeans came.

Among the Hausa-Fulani and the Kanuri and others in Northern Nigeria, there were strong states under traditional rulers including emirs and the Sardauna of Sokoto who wielded so much power that he became the most powerful leader in Nigeria even after the country won independence because the federation was dominated by Northern Nigeria which was under his control.

The Igbo were the exception among the three largest ethnic groups which constitute Nigeria's triad – the Hausa-Fulani in the north, the Yoruba in the west, and the Igbo in the east. They did not have central authority.

The imposition of colonial rule on the Igbo was the first time state formation took place among them, uniting them under the British administrators, unlike in other parts of Nigeria where the people were already united under their traditional rulers.

There was also the kingdom of Benin, or the Edo empire, in what is now southern Nigeria, one of the most powerful in precolonial Africa. The king of Benin ruled as an absolute monarch, thus leading one of the most centralised states in precolonial Africa.

There were others in different parts of the continent.

In the former Belgian Congo, the Bakongo were organised in a powerful kingdom, one of the best organised on the continent, and after which two countries were named.

It covered a vast expanse of territory not only in what

is now the Democratic Republic of Congo (the former Belgian Congo) and the Republic of Congo (Congo-Brazzaville) but also a part of Angola in northern Cabinda.

It was ruled by one king, *Mwene Kongo*, and exerted influence on other kingdoms in the region. And it was not the only kingdom or state in that part of Africa before Europeans came.

What came to be known as Angola under Portuguese rule also had kingdoms – well-organised states – before Africa was invaded and conquered by Europeans. Some of the most well-known were Ndongo and Matamba.

In the western part of what came to be Northern Rhodesia, now Zambia, in a region called Barotseland, the Lozi built a kingdom in precolonial times.

It was one of the most successful on the continent in the precolonial era, having united at least 25 different ethnic groups including members of the northern Sotho tribe of South Africa who migrated there and were assimilated by the Barotse and became Barotse themselves.

Members of other tribes who became Barotse migrated from Congo, Namibia, Angola, Zimbabwe and South Africa. The original founders of the kingdom came from Congo, what became the Belgian Congo during colonial rule.

During its heyday, the Barotse empire stretched into South West Africa, now Namibia, and into Angola as well as other parts of what is now Zambia. The king of Barotseland was known as *litunga*.

In modern Botswana, formerly Bechuanaland when it was ruled by Britain, there were a number of states before colonial rule. One of the most well-known was the Bamangwato whose hereditary rulers – kings – included Seretse Khama who became the first president of Botswana after the country won independence. He became *kgosi* (king) of his people before independence. He was the grandson of Khama III, king of the Bamangwato.

There was the Swazi kingdom in precolonial times which continued to exist during colonial rule. After independence, it continued to be known as the Kingdom of Swaziland and is now officially called Eswatini or the Kingdom of Eswatini.

In what is now Mozambique, the Gaza kingdom, also known as the Gaza empire, covered a large area in the southern part of the country and southeastern Zimbabwe and extended into the northern part of South Africa.

The Yao of northern Mozambique in Niassa Province built some of the most powerful kingdoms and states in East Africa. They straddle the Tanzanian-Mozambican border. They are also found in large numbers in Malawi where two presidents, Bakili Muluzi, and Joyce Banda who was the country's first female president and one of the first in Africa, were Yao.

The Maravi kingdom, after which the country of Malawi is named, covered a vast expanse of territory in the areas of what is now Malawi, Mozambique and Zambia. It was a confederacy, a form of union in which constituent parts enjoy extensive autonomy.

In South Africa was the Zulu kingdom established by Shaka. It became one of the most powerful and best organised, militarily, in the history of precolonial Africa.

There was also the kingdom of Zimbabwe in southern Africa, a kingdom founded by the Shona and other ethnic groups which covered a vast expanse of territory extending beyond the borders of what is now the country of Zimbabwe, formerly Southern Rhodesia.

There were other states in the area of modern Zimbabwe including the kingdom of Mapungubwe located south of the kingdom of Great Zimbabwe and which played a major role in the formation of the kingdom of Zimbabwe.

There was also the Bukalanga kingdom which, like many others on the continent, was multi-ethnic composed of the Bakalanga of what is now northeastern Botswana, the Karanga of western Zimbabwe, and the Venda of the northeastern part of modern South Africa.

Like other Africans, the indigenous people of what is now Zimbabwe, the Shona and the Ndebele, fiercely resisted the imperial forces when Southern Rhodesia was being formed as a colony,

The Ndebele established a powerful state in the southern part of what is now the country of Zimbabwe. It was a highly centralised state under the leadership of Mzilikazi, its founder. He broke away from Shaka in what is Kwazulu-Natal Province today and fled north with his people, finally settling in what became the British colony of Southern Rhodesia.

During their last resistance against the British, the Ndebele were led by Lobengula, the son of Mzilikazi and their last king, who summed up the duplicitous nature of their conquerors in these poignant words:

"Do you know how a chameleon catches a fly?

It gets behind the fly, remains motionless for some time, then advances very slowly and gently, first putting forward one leg and then another. At last, when well within reach, it darts its tongue and the fly disappears. England is the chameleon and I am the fly."

Those are just some examples of the traditional states which existed in precolonial Africa. And where no complex systems of government in the form of a state existed, there were chiefdoms or other forms of central authority uniting the people under one leadership; which was also a form of government even if it did not fit the definition of government the way the colonial rulers defined it.

It was government, nonetheless, and served Africans well. Africans were not happy they were conquered and colonised. And they were not happy they had to pay taxes to be ruled by other people – from Europe or anywhere else.

Some of the kingdoms and empires in different parts of the continent disintegrated but later evolved into other political units, highly organised states comprising different ethnic groups under one leadership as multi-ethnic entities or as individual ethnic groups.

Many ethnic groups simply had chiefdoms including some of the most powerful in their regions. They included the Hehe of Tanzania whose chief, Mkwawa, led his people in a fierce war against the German colonial rulers in his homeland in the Southern Highlands. It was one the most heroic wars in the history of the country, together with the Maji Maji war of resistance from 1905 to 1907 which almost ended German rule.

In 1891, Mkwawa's army of 3,000 soldiers overpowered the German colonial force and killed its commander, Emil von Zelewski. In retaliation, the Germans launched a major attack on Mkwawa's fortress at Kalenga in 1894 but could not capture him. He escaped and continued to wage guerrilla warfare against the colonial forces until 1898 when he shot himself. He vowed he was not going to be captured alive. He is a nationalist hero in Tanzania.

The Germans also cut off his head and took the skull to Germany. It was returned to Tanganyika in 1954, coincidentally in the same year the nationalist campaign for independence started in earnest when the party that led the independence struggle, the Tanganyika African national union (TANU), was formed.

All these examples of precolonial states, empires, kingdoms and chiefdoms clearly show that Africans did not learn from Europeans how to form nations and governments. They already existed when Europeans arrived.

Still, a case can be made that colonisation, or colonial rule, was responsible for state formation in Africa – but *only if* it is acknowledged that the colonial rulers destroyed what we already had and replaced it with theirs; not that they built states because none existed before they came.

An argument can also be made that the colonised got some benefits *not* from colonialism but from the things the colonisers did to facilitate imperial rule; which is not a defence of colonialism.

The colonial rulers were responsible for state formation which led to the creation of the countries we have in Africa today. They united different ethnic groups – smaller tribal states – to form larger administrative entities we inherited at independence and on which we continued to build our nations.

There was no Tanganyika or Nigeria or any of the other countries on the continent ruled by Europeans before the advent of colonial rule.

That does *not* mean the colonisers formed those countries to help or benefit Africans. They created them to facilitate imperial rule and help themselves and their mother countries.

Yet, Africans benefited from the creation of those nations – the ones we have today – which did not exist before but instead had tribal units which for all practical purposes are the units they identified with and to which they pledged allegiance as their nations.

Most Africans don't want to break up the countries we have today and return to precolonial days to live under tribal authorities which constituted states of their tribal nations during those days.

What they demand is inclusive government, meaningful participation in decision making and in the political process, and democratic representation in institutions of authority without excluding some groups; an exclusion which has led to demands for extensive autonomy or devolution of power and even secession.

But they prefer to live in the larger political units and be members of the nations we have today – Ghana,

Zambia, Kenya and so on – which were formed by the colonial rulers.

That does not mean those political units – colonial territories, now our countries – were created to help Africans pursue unity in the name of Pan-African solidarity.

They were created to facilitate colonial rule, in most cases by centralising authority and by administering through indirect rule, a system introduced by Lord Lugard in Northern Nigeria. Yet Nigeria was not created to benefit Africans living within the boundaries of what came to be the Nigerian federation. It was created for the purpose of exploitation to benefit the colonial power: Britain.

Still, Nigerians benefited from the existence of Nigeria as a single political entity they inherited at independence instead of breaking it up into smaller political units – the tribal states – which existed before colonial rule. And that was the case in all the other former colonies across the continent.

None of them decided to break up and return to tribal rule, with each tribe or ethnic group having its own authority as an independent and separate political unit.

African leaders agreed in May 1963 when they met in Addis Ababa, Ethiopia, and formed the Organisation of African Unity (OAU) that they would maintain the boundaries they inherited at independence. It was Nyerere who presented that resolution. As he stated in what amounted to a farewell speech to Africa – not long before he died – he delivered in an informal way at the University of Dar es Salaam on 15 December 1997:

"I was responsible for moving that resolution that Africa must accept the borders, which we inherited from colonialism; accept them as they are. That resolution was passed by the organisation (OAU) with two reservations: one from Morocco, another from Somalia.

Let me say why I moved that resolution.

In 1960, just before this country became independent, I think I was then chief minister; I received a delegation of Masai elders from Kenya, led by an American missionary. And they came to persuade me to let the Masai invoke something called the Anglo-Masai Agreement so that that section of the Masai in Kenya should become part of Tanganyika; so that when Tanganyika becomes independent, it includes part of Masai, from Kenya.

I suspected the American missionary was responsible for that idea. I don't remember that I was particularly polite to him.

Kenyatta was then in detention, and here somebody comes to me, that we should break up Kenya and make part of Kenya part of Tanganyika. But why shouldn't Kenyatta demand that the Masai part of Tanganyika should become Masai of Kenya? It's the same logic. That was in 1960.

In 1961 we became independent. In 1962, early 1962, I resigned as prime minister and then a few weeks later I received Dr. Banda. *Mungu amuweke mahali pema* (May God rest his soul in peace). I received Dr. Banda. We had just, FRELIMO had just been established here and we were now in the process of starting the armed struggle.

So Banda comes to me with a big old book, with lots and lots of maps in it, and tells me, 'Mwalimu, what is this, what is Mozambique? There is no such thing as Mozambique.' I said, 'What do you mean there is no such thing as Mozambique?'

So he showed me this map, and he said: 'That part is part of Nyasaland (it was still Nyasaland, not Malawi, at that time). That part is part of Southern Rhodesia, That part is Swaziland, and this part, which is the northern part, Makonde part, that is *your* part.'

So Banda disposed of Mozambique just like that. I ridiculed the idea, and Banda never liked anybody to ridicule his ideas. So he left and went to Lisbon to talk to Salazar about this wonderful idea. I don't know what

Salazar told him. That was '62.

In '63 we go to Addis Ababa for the inauguration of the OAU, and Ethiopia and Somalia are at war over the Ogaden. We had to send a special delegation to bring the president of Somalia to attend that inaugural summit, because the two countries were at *war.* Why? Because Somalia wanted the Ogaden, a *whole* province of Ethiopia, saying, 'That is part of Somalia.' And Ethiopia was quietly, the Emperor quietly saying to us that 'the whole of Somalia is part of Ethiopia.'

So those three, the delegation of the Masai, led by the American missionary; Banda's old book of maps; and the Ogaden, caused me to move that resolution, in Cairo 1964. And I say, the resolution was accepted, two countries with reservations, and one was Somalia because Somalia wanted the Ogaden; Somalia wanted northern Kenya; Somalia wanted Djibouti." – (Julius K. Nyerere, at an international conference at the University of Dar es Salaam, Tanzania, December 15, 1997. The transcription of the non-written speech came from Mrs. Magombe of the Nyerere Foundation, Dar es Salaam. Translation of Kiswahili words, phrases and sentences in Nyerere's speech into English in the preceding text, done by the author, Godfrey Mwakikagile. Reproduced in Godfrey Mwakikagile, *Nyerere and Africa: End of an Era*, Pretoria, South Africa: New Africa Press, 2010, pp. 556 – 557).

Maintaining colonial borders inherited at independence helped maintain peace in Africa which would have been threatened had the newly independent states challenged the legitimacy of those boundaries at the expense of their neighbours to fulfill their expansionist ambitions by invoking dubious and conflicting land rights based on ethnic identities and boundaries of precolonial times.

The colonial authorities did, of course, do more than just draw boundaries and unite – more than separate – many ethnic groups to create colonial entities or territories which became their colonies.

With state formation by the colonial powers came other developments including the establishment of schools, hospitals, transport networks – roads and railways – and other institutions and facilities of modernisation. Again, this was done mainly to facilitate colonial rule more than anything else.

The colonial rulers did not even build many hospitals and clinics. Post-colonial governments in some countries – such as Ghana under Nkrumah and Tanzania under Nyerere – built more hospitals and other medical facilities than the colonial rulers did.

Some countries also expanded the transport network and built other infrastructure which did not exist before colonial rule. Some of them also built factories to manufacture import-substitution items and other products. The colonial rulers never intended to build them because they wanted all manufactured goods imported from their home countries – Africa being used only as a market for imports from the metropolitan powers – and from a few "favoured" colonies such as Kenya whose exports went to neighbouring Uganda and Tanganyika.

The schools the colonial governments built were also not enough to train the required number of people our countries would need to meet their manpower requirements after they won independence. They built only enough to meet their needs – educate a limited number of Africans to work for the colonial governments even though the money to fund those schools came from the Africans themselves: the taxes they paid and the money the colonial governments earned from cash crops grown by African farmers but for which they were grossly underpaid by the colonial rulers.

Also, the limited higher education Africans were able to obtain was mainly a product of their effort. They demanded to be educated while the colonial rulers wanted to provide only lower education for clerical work and other services needed to maintain colonial rule.

Even church schools – established by European missionaries – were funded by the Africans themselves from the contributions they made to their churches yet did not get their money's worth in terms of education and other services.

After African countries won independence, they built far more schools and trained far more people in a much shorter period than the colonial rulers did during a much longer period they ruled those countries. As Nyerere stated at a meeting with World Bank officials in Washington, D.C., in 1997:

"We took over a country with 85 per cent of its adults illiterate. The British ruled us for 42 years. When they left, there were two trained engineers and 12 doctors. When I stepped down, there was 91 per cent literacy and nearly every child was in school. We trained thousands of engineers, doctors and teachers." – (Julius K. Nyerere, quoted by Godfrey Mwakikagile, *Nyerere and Africa: End of an Era*, op. cit., p. 76; Julius Nyerere, quoted in *Sunday Times*, London, October 3, 1999; R.W. Johnson, "Nyerere: A Flawed Hero," *The National Interest*, June 1, 2000, Washington, D.C., p. 73. See also, "Farewell to the Father of Tanzania," in the *Mail and Guardian*, Johannesburg, October 15, 1999; "Julius Nyerere of Tanzania Dies; Preached African Socialism to the World," in *The New York Times*, October 15, 1999, p. B10; "Former Tanzanian President Julius Nyerere Dies at 77; African leader Led Independence Movement and Worked to Unify Nation, Continent," in *The Washington Post*, October 15, 1999, p. B-06; "Julius Nyerere: Former President of Tanzania Led Country to Independence," in the *Los Angeles Times*, October 15, 1999, p. 30).

That was great achievement within 24 years he was president. He stepped down in November 1985.

Even the way the roads and railways were built clearly showed they were intended to facilitate exploitation of African resources in the interior and other parts of the colonies. They went straight to where the resources were. The resources – minerals and other commodities such as tea, coffee, cocoa cotton and forestry products – were transported from the interior to the coast to be shipped to Europe. Areas which had no resources to be exploited were ignored in terms of "development." They hardly had any roads or modern facilities built by the colonial governments.

When our countries won independence, they inherited the transport network and other infrastructure although none was built to benefit Africans – in fact, it was African labourers who built all the infrastructure, earning meagre wages and sometimes nothing or just a simple meal now and then.

State formation – the creation of modern institutions of authority as well as the countries we have today in Africa – by the imperial powers also facilitated our integration into the international community. We effectively became an integral part of it unlike before when we were virtually isolated.

The educational system – schools built by the colonial rulers and European missionaries – also played a major role in laying the foundation of our modern sates even though the primary purpose of building those schools was to train Africans to work for the colonial governments and facilitate imperial rule.

Imposition of imperial rule on us meant we were no longer the owners of our own homeland. For all practical purposes, Africans no longer owned Africa during colonial rule.

We not only became captives in our own motherland, of all places; we lost the only place that was home to us.

We were even given new names by our conquerors – Gold Coast, Ivory Coast, Rhodesia, Nigeria, Niger, Central

African Republic, Sierra Leone, Cameroon, Guinea, Deutsch-Ostafrika (German East Africa), Deutsch-Südwestafrika (German South West Africa), Transvaal, Natal, and so on.

Even some of our lakes and mountains were named after our European conquerors, replacing indigenous names: Lake Victoria instead of Nyanza; Lake Albert, Victoria Falls, Livingstone Mountains, Drakensberg Mountains, Murchison Falls.

So were towns and cities: Leopoldville, Stanleyville, Elisabethville, Albertville in Belgian Congo; Brazzaville in French Congo (Congo-Brazzaville), Libreville in Gabon, Livingstone in Northern Rhodesia, Francistown in Bechuanaland, Eldoret in Kenya, Salisbury in Southern Rhodesia, Lagos in Nigeria; Grahamstown, Durban, Cape Town, Port Elizabeth, Pretoria, Johannesburg, Bloemfontein in South Africa; Blantyre in Nyasaland; Lourenço Marques, Beira in Mozambique; Walvis Bay, Windhoek, South West Africa (Namibia), Cape Coast in the Gold Coast, Broken Hill in Northern Rhodesia, Neu Langenburg in Deutsch-Ostafrika (Tanganyika).

By doing so, the colonial rulers erased the history of many places which was preserved and transmitted by the use of indigenous names.

Colonisation also not only robbed us of our natural right to live free and think for ourselves; it also robbed us of our dignity and self-esteem. We were reduced to being mere objects of ridicule and contempt.

In the eyes of our conquerors, we even ceased to be full human beings – if we ever were, to them.

There is no question that the colonisation of Africa has had a profound impact on the personality of Africans as individuals and as a collective entity in a way no other external force or form of invasion has had on the continent. And its effects are still felt and manifested in many ways even today.

Conquest of our ancestors by the imperial powers can

be attributed to one thing: weakness. This weakness can also be attributed to something else: lack of technological development. Without technology, Africans could not make advanced weapons to defend themselves against the superior firepower of the invaders from Europe.

The invaders had guns – Africans did not – enabling only a few European soldiers and adventurers to conquer vast expanses of territory inhabited by millions of people. Simply firing a few bullets or a single cannon, with its "sonic boom," was enough – in fact more than enough – to scare and scatter the "natives" and send them running for their lives with their spears, bows and arrows.

The conquest of Africa was that simple in terms of firepower. Africans fighting Europeans was a mismatch. The imperial order prevailed, thanks to European guns. This is what Professor Kenneth Minogue, in his book *Nationalism*, calls the technological theory of imperialism, expressed in jingoistic terms: "We have got, the Gatling gun, and they have not."

The Gatling gun played a major role in intimidating, subduing and conquering Africans during the era of colonisation; its firepower best demonstrated during the Anglo-Ashanti wars in the Gold Coast, the Anglo-Zulu wars in South Africa, and against the Ndebele in Southern Rhodesia. And it happened the same way in other parts of Africa where our Europeans conquerors used guns, or the mere threat of it, to subjugate the "natives."

The rest of the Africans in those regions got the message which spread fast farther afield, itself as a weapon of psychological conquest of the people. They were conquered even before they could think of resisting invasion or they simply surrendered, knowing the odds against them, because of European guns whose use was the best expression of imperial might. And that had a profound impact on us as a people. We were emasculated.

The psychological wounds inflicted on us by our conquerors caused enormous and incalculable damage in terms of self-esteem and even personality formation and development among some of our people who came to believe that our conquest could be best explained in terms of natural differences between blacks and whites; that whites were more technologically advanced and more powerful than we were because they were naturally superior to us. For, how else could we explain our defeat and humiliation by a mere handful of whites, here and there, when they invaded us? Even if this could be explained in terms of guns, why were we not able to make them before they came and when we were fighting them if we had the same mental capacity to do so? And why are they so far ahead of us even today?

While some of us – including me in my book *Africa is in a Mess: What Went Wrong and What Should Be Done* – do concede there have indeed been some benefits from the interaction that has taken place between Africa and Europe through the centuries, and that the benefits have been reciprocal not just one-sided as our conquerors and their supporters amongst us claim that we have been the biggest beneficiaries because of Western material civilisation that was brought to us, history is not on their side and their admirers among us.

It took Europe hundreds of years to develop and get where they are today; much of that development attributed to other cultures including Africa.

Europeans did not invent the wheel on which many civilisations have rolled forward since its invention. They did not develop arithmetic critical to scientific progress and technological development; nor did they invent gunpowder which was vital to Europe's conquest of other cultures and civilisations.

Even Africa's contribution to Europe's development in terms of material and labour – the two being the most obvious from the time they conquered us although our intellectual contribution before then and after cannot be ignored – far exceeds what Europe contributed to the development of Africa.

Yet Africa's contribution to the development of Europe and Europe's role in the underdevelopment of Africa is hardly acknowledged by our conquerors because they were the beneficiaries of both. And they still are in this era of globalisation.

There is little in Europe's argument – that European countries initiated and fuelled their own development – that can refute or undermine Walter Rodney's thesis of his work, *How Europe Underdeveloped Africa.*

Europe's contribution to Africa's development has been extraction: building extractive industries – for minerals and other resources – to benefit Europe. And that still goes on today. Look at who benefits the most from the exploitation of Africa's natural wealth including land, not just minerals and others resources.

By its very nature, colonisation is exploitative – and oppressive to facilitate exploitation. Oppression goes hand in hand with degradation to strip the colonised of their dignity in order to make them submissive and easy to dominate them.

Recolonisation of Africa has become the norm in this era of globalisation. It is even lauded by some brainwashed Africans as our only salvation from the misery and suffering, and grinding poverty, tens of millions of our people have to endure all their lives.

Even during colonial rule, the disadvantages of colonisation far outweighed its advantages. Most of the advantages have been the result of mutual cooperation between the two – Africa and Europe – although in a lopsided way, with Europe benefiting more than Africa has from this interaction.

But because we were conquered and subjugated, it is difficult if not impossible for some of our people to acknowledge all that even if they know it is true.

Europe has not been our saviour; very much to the contrary. Our very African-ness has been sorely tested by this European invasion whose impact continues to shape the destiny of many Africans including entire nations despite years of "independence" from alien rule.

Yet we know who and what we are, the essence of our very being, rooted in traditional Africa. It is this essence of African-ness which is acknowledged even by some Westernised or brainwashed Africans in rare moments of nostalgia when they say: That is how we lived before the coming of Europeans; that is how our ancestors lived; that is what our ancestors did; not everything was good but they were good old days; our communal and family ties were stronger then than they are now; that is how we lived as Africans – an that is what it meant to be African. Sadly, those days are gone.

It was an essence, of African-ness, that was not contaminated or threatened in its pristine beauty, by foreign influence, because there was no such influence. When Westernised Africans acknowledge this essence, they are invoking the essence of their very being. Yet, they at the same repudiate it when they embrace Westernisation or any other foreign influence and identity because they think it is better than being African.

It does not mean we want to isolate and insulate ourselves from the rest of the world. We can continue to be active members of the global community, learn from others as much as they can learn from us, and benefit from modernisation without losing or compromising our identity and essence as Africans. And that means reclaiming the spirit and values of traditional Africa and its institutions as well as indigenous knowledge to enable us to chart our way forward and navigate in the treacherous waters of globalisation which threaten the integrity and wellbeing of Africa in terms of identity and personality.

We have to be what we are. Otherwise we are going to copy everything from other people and become a product of other cultures as if we did not have our own essence and identity before we came into contact with them. It would be as if we never even existed before.

We cannot abandon or denigrate our cultural identity. Without culture, our own culture, we are nothing as a people. Culture is not only a vital force and source of life for a nation, any nation, and for Africa as a collective entity even if it is not a monolithic whole; it is its very definition. Africa is organic in essence, with a vital force of its own that animates it and gives it a distinctive identity.

By turning against traditional Africa, modernised Africans have not only turned against themselves; they have lost their soul since it is traditional Africa which is the essence of their very being.

There is no question that cultural imperialism has had a devastating impact on many Africans in terms of identity. Many of them prefer to be anything else – and everything else – but African. That is because they are ashamed of who they are and what they are. They are ashamed of their "primitive" African heritage; they are ashamed of Africa's "backwardness" – and even the food our people eat in villages and prefer European food because they are "civilised."

Some of them are even proud to say they have "forgotten" their native languages after living outside Africa, especially in Europe, the United States and other non-African countries, preferably "white," for only a few years; sometimes for only two to three – let alone five or more.

They say they can no longer speak Kiswahili; they can no longer speak Gikuyu (Kikuyu), Chinyanja, Shona, Mende – the list goes on and on. They can only speak English, French, German, Dutch, Swedish, Polish, Spanish or some other European language. Many of them have not even mastered those languages. Yet they are so proud of them simply because they are not African languages.

There are even those who anglicise their African names or spell them in some other European language they speak.

Why not? It makes them "sophisticated," "civilised," "educated," "Europeanised" – and no longer "backward," "primitive" and "uncivilised."

Many Africans also like to mix English, French or Portuguese – the languages of our former colonial masters – with the native languages they speak as a sign of being "sophisticated" and "educated," a phenomenon which, in East Africa, has led to the evolution of what we call Kiswanglish, a hybrid of Kiswahili and English especially in Kenya and Tanzania.

That is very common among the elite, most of whom are a product of Western education. That is the case even in local schools in terms of intellectual preparation from primary school patterned after the colonial educational systems we inherited and are therefore Western because that is where our rulers came from.

Even our countries are described as "English-speaking," "French-speaking" or "Portuguese-speaking" even though the vast majority of our people in those countries don't even understand or speak those languages. Many of them don't even want to learn those languages. They are satisfied with what they already know – their own native languages.

Africans themselves describe our countries in terms of being "Anglophone," "Francophone" and "Lusophone" instead of describing them as being multi-lingual African-speaking countries since most of the people in those countries speak their own native languages, not European languages.

They don't even want to become "European" like many of their educated brethren who try to be more "European" than the Europeans themselves by desperately trying to shed or run away from their African identity.

"Uneducated" Africans and those who live in villages are more African than their educated brothers and sisters – some of whom don't even know what they really are, caught between two worlds, African and non-African.

They are caught between being a part of Africa or Europe, Africa or America and so on.

And the less African they become, by identifying with and becoming a part of the non-African world and deliberately distancing themselves from their African identity and heritage, the prouder they are.

That has been one of the devastating results and consequences of our being colonised – subjugated and brainwashed by our conquerors into believing that any other place, especially Europe and any other part of the "white" world, is better than Africa.

Cultural imperialism also has been very destructive in terms of indigenous knowledge.

Our indigenous knowledge has been lost through the suppression of our native languages which are the repository of knowledge transmitted from one generation to the next.

It is a tragedy that the languages of our conquerors who ruled us are the preferred languages in our countries, especially by the elite and government officials and leaders. They are still given priority at the expense of our native languages even decades after independence as if we want to remain under European control and are proud of being an extension of Europe.

In most African countries, very little or nothing is being done to give native languages priority and the status they deserve as vital tools for the preservation and dissemination of indigenous knowledge and as a vital part of our identity while, at the same time, continuing to use the languages of the former colonial powers – English, French and Portuguese as well as Spanish in former Spanish Guinea, now Equatorial Guinea – out of necessity.

It is as if our native languages are irrelevant to our wellbeing as Africans, reinforcing the notion, and the attitude as well as the perception, that nothing good comes out of Africa except gold, diamonds and other minerals and resources. And nothing good – not even indigenous knowledge and institutions – ever came from Africans except labour, especially manual labour extracted from Africans in conditions which amounted to virtual slavery and even outright enslavement to serve our conquerors.

Although we have benefited from the knowledge that we have obtained from the West through schools established by our colonial rulers and missionaries, there is no question that Western education was also intended to de-Africanise Africans.

Even educated Africans deliberately attempted to de-Africanise themselves by turning against their own indigenous cultures and traditional ways of life and values – and therefore turned against their own very being – in order to become "British," "French," and "Portuguese," the colonial powers which ruled Africa.

Western education was also intended to alienate educated Africans from their own people – the more educated they were, the less African they became – and turn them into loyal servants of our conquerors to perpetuate imperial domination of Africa even after the end of colonial rule; a goal that was achieved in most cases as has been demonstrated by the existence of neo-colonial governments and institutions in all parts of the continent since independence, making a mockery of the sacrifices we made to end colonial rule.

There were only a few exceptions where neo-colonialism faced stiff resistance. That was in Ghana under Nkrumah, Tanzania under Nyerere, and Guinea under Sekou Toure. The three leaders were also ideological compatriots who earned Africa a respectable place in the global arena as relentless and uncompromising champions of African liberation, unity and independence. And they never wavered even when the positions they took were challenged by the leaders of powerful nations, especially Western, on a number of vital and fundamental issues affecting the wellbeing of Africa and the Third World as a whole.

They made genuine attempts to achieve true independence.

But even in those countries, there were subversive elements within the government and elsewhere in society who collaborated with the imperialist powers to undermine the leaders and subvert institutions of authority in order to sabotage their efforts to achieve true liberation from foreign domination, especially Western.

In fact, we have witnessed a sad spectacle since the end of colonial rule in the sixties when most African countries won independence: the collapse of a number of states in different parts of the continent because of bad leadership around which everything else revolves.

The vast majority of the leaders we have had since independence have been corrupt, incompetent, despotic and tribalist – a liability imperial powers have effectively exploited to establish and support neo-colonial governments and institutions.

So, we see that the colonial rulers never really left Africa; they only changed faces. There is no other way to look at it unless we want to delude ourselves into believing that we achieved genuine independence and are truly free today, while the rest of the world laughs at us for being so stupid to believe that – as if we are a bunch of idiots to whom naïveté is a virtue to be glorified and celebrated.

And that would justify the psychological defeat we also suffered at the hands of our conquerors when they conquered our minds as well.

We have been victims of imperial conquest from the beginning when our conquerors invaded our continent for the first time as soon as they arrived from Europe to colonise us. We are still their victims even today. And we were conquered in more than one way.

We lost our land. We lost our freedom, We lost our dignity and self-esteem. We even lost our mind, "the mind of Africa," to use Dr. Willie Abraham's phrase which is also the title of his highly philosophical work, when we were brainwashed by our conquerors into believing they were superior to us in terms of intelligence and everything else. Not all of us believed that. But many of our people did and still do. We lost terribly. The list goes on and on.

But we did not lose our humanity and our intrinsic worth of being humane more than our conquerors were.

Still, we were conquered. Our capacity to be humane did not save us; in fact, it was a liability and our downfall in many areas when dealing with our invaders who did not care about morality except when it benefited them. We also fought back, of course, and still lost mainly because of our technological inferiority. We should admit that.

But it was *conquest of the mind* where we suffered ultimate defeat. Conquest of the mind was the worst form of imperial subjugation whose impact is still felt today. Many of our people have been thoroughly brainwashed by our conquerors.

Even when we try to find solutions to our problems, we look to Europe and America – or some other non-African country, especially white – for guidance and assistance instead of looking within Africa itself to find those solutions from our own people.

We are so dependent on other people – they even have to build buildings for us including the headquarters of the African Union (AU), of all buildings – that we even refuse to think for ourselves, and don't want to think for ourselves, to find solutions to our own problems. Yet these are African problems, within Africa itself, and should and *do* have African solutions.

But because we are a conquered people, even mentally and psychologically, we have to turn to our conquerors – of all people – to help us as if they are a part of us and we are a part of them. And this didn't just start. It started from the beginning when they conquered us and consolidated their rule over us through the years when we were under colonial rule.

It has been a tragic history for us as a conquered people. Our subservience to our former colonial masters and other powers we always beg to help us has been ruthlessly public – in the international spotlight – for decades since independence.

Even our annual budgets have to be approved by them although most of the money does not come from them but comes from our own resources within.

Our leaders worry about what the leaders of powerful nations think about our condition and the problems we face instead of worrying about our own people – what they think and what they have to say; although leaders of powerful nations don't even care about us – they couldn't care less. But they are the ones we always beg to help us in almost all areas of national life. Therefore, our leaders have to listen to them, and in a subservient way, as they continue to beg. We beg too much, far more than people in other continents do.

That is the history of conquest and the psychology of conquered people.

In many cases during colonial rule, the conquered even ended up identifying with their conquerors. They emulated them. They not only tried to be more British than the British themselves, or more French than the French themselves; they wanted to be "white."

They glorified our conquerors as if they were the best specimen of mankind in spite of all the suffering and humiliation they inflicted on them.

That also has been the case with many of our people since independence, including those who were born after independence. Many of them look to the West – where our conquerors came from – for guidance; although this can also partly be attributed to rotten leadership across Africa during the post-colonial era because our leaders have failed to address our problems the way they should have.

The psychological defeat we suffered at the hands of our conquerors turned many of our people against themselves, against their African-ness.

Many of them even today want to be "white" in every conceivable way. Some of them even bleach their skin in a desperate attempt to change their physical appearance and shed their African identity. The lighter, the better – that is the "whiter" the better.

It is sad, depressingly sad, that many Africans have also chosen our former colonial rulers to be their "kith-kin" instead of embracing their own people, fellow Africans, as their true kith-and-kin.

They identify themselves with their former colonial masters more than they do with fellow Africans who were ruled by other colonial powers. For example, Guineans, Malians and Senegalese identify with the French more than they do with Ghanaians, Nigerians and Sierra Leoneans who were ruled by the British, further reinforcing the racist notion that Europeans are superior to Africans – it is better to be a part of them than it is to be a part of fellow Africans.

This political and cultural divide between Francophone and Anglophone Africa is evident even in the African Union (AU), an umbrella organisation who primary objective is to foster African solidarity and cooperation in solving and finding solutions to African problems including disunity among ourselves. Yet it has done exactly the opposite in terms of fostering unity. Despite professions to the contrary, the African Union is operating under the banner of "us versus them" when Pan-African solidarity and unity is being pursued.

There is rivalry and even mistrust between member countries which were ruled by the two colonial powers: France and Britain. And that has been the case since the Organisation of African Unity (OAU) – which preceded the AU – was formed in Addis Ababa, Ethiopia, in May 1963 whose only achievement was in supporting the African liberation movements fighting to end white minority rule in the countries of southern Africa and

Portuguese Guinea in West Africa. It was a tragic failure in conflict resolution, let alone in pursing the goal of continental unity under one government.

In terms of Franco-British – or British-French – rivalry in post-colonial Africa, the most tragic case and glaring example within a country is the civil conflict – which has been bloody – between Anglophone Cameroon and Francophone Cameroon in a nation where the former colonial power, France, still wields enormous power and influence, and is virtually the final arbiter on all matters, to the detriment of English-speaking Cameroonians of Southern Cameroons (comprising the Northwest Region and the Southwest Region of the Republic of Cameroon) who constitute what should at least be an autonomous entity in a genuine federation or confederation or even an independent state if that is the only way the conflict can be resolved.

It is not unusual for the former colonial powers to intervene in conflicts in their former colonies or simply to interfere in their affairs because they still consider them to be their spheres of influence.

Imperial control of Africa is manifested in many other ways, making a mockery of independence Africans are so proud of. It is as if our struggle for independence amounted to nothing and we want to return to the status quo ante and be a part of the old colonial empires.

One of the tragedies that befell Africa was that to many Africans, our conquerors – European colonial rulers and settlers – not only became their role models; they emulated them in many ways and and as much as they could. By doing so, they ended up destroying themselves. It was diminution of African identity and a brutal attack on the African personality. And it still goes on even today, as many Africans try to run away from themselves and be what they are not.

All that is clear victory for cultural imperialism. Evidence is everywhere, not only in terms of language –

English and French are the main official languages in Africa – but also in terms of cultural imitation with many Africans adopting European manners and mannerisms as well as cultures. It is also a victory in terms of ideas propagated by the West to our detriment as if we cannot think for ourselves.

Yet that is exactly what we fought for: not only to end colonial rule – only to invite our former rulers back – but to rule ourselves and think for ourselves for our own wellbeing. And let the people decide.

We never had the opportunity to decide for ourselves during colonial rule on a wide range of issues affecting our wellbeing and destiny as one people constituting a nation; our colonial masters did that for us. Sadly, even today, most of our leaders across the continent don't allow the people to decide for themselves decades after colonial rule ended.

The end of colonial rule came with responsibilities. The main responsibility was for us to be responsible for ourselves and for our own wellbeing. That is still the case today. Nobody is going to help us. We should not even want or expect other people to solve our problems. We have to help ourselves. Otherwise our independence is meaningless. And that seems to be the case.

We should not expect other people to come to our rescue or solve our problems. We are on our own. The rest of the world does *not* care about us. And it shouldn't when we don't care enough about ourselves and don't do enough to help ourselves to solve our own problems. As Nyerere said in his speech at the University of Dar es Salaam, Tanzania, which was conversational in tone and style, not long before he died:

"You wanted me to reflect. I told you I had very little time to reflect. I am not an engineer (reference to the vice-chancellor of the University of Dar es Salaam who identified himself as an engineer in his introductory remarks) and therefore what I am going to say might sound messy, unstructured and possibly irrelevant to what you intend to do; but I thought that if by reflecting, you wanted me to go back and relive the political life that I have lived for the last 30, 40 years, that I cannot do.

And in any case, in spite of the fact that it's useful to go back in history, what you are talking about is what might be of use to Africa in the 21st century. History's important, obviously, but I think we should concentrate and see what might be of use to our continent in the coming century.

What I want to do is share with you some thoughts on two issues concerning Africa. One, an obvious one; when I speak, you will realise how obvious it is. Another one, less obvious, and I'll spend a little more time on the less obvious one, because I think this will put Africa in what is going to be Africa's context in the 21st century. And the new leadership of Africa will have to concern itself with the situation in which it finds itself in the world tomorrow – in the world of the 21st century. And the Africa I'm going to be talking about, is Africa south of the Sahara, sub-Saharan Africa. I'll explain later the reason why I chose to concentrate on Africa south of the Sahara. It is because of the point I want to emphasise.

It appears today that in the world tomorrow, there are going to be three centres of power: some, political power; some, economic power, but three centres of real power in the world.

One centre is the United States of America and Canada; what you call North America. That is going to be a huge economic power, and probably for a long time the only military power, but a huge economic power.

The other one is going to be Western Europe, another huge economic power. I think Europe is choosing deliberately not to be a military power. I think they deliberately want to leave that to the United States.

The other one is Japan. Japan is in a different category

but it is better to say Japan, because the power of Japan is quite clear, the economic power of Japan is obvious.

The three powers are going to affect the countries near them.

I was speaking in South Africa recently and I referred to Mexico. A former president of Mexico, I think it must have been after the revolution in 1935, no, after the revolution; a former president of Mexico is reported to have complained about his country or lamented about his country. 'Poor Mexico,' said the president, 'so far from God yet so near the United States.' He was complaining about the disadvantages of being a neighbour of a giant.

Today, Mexico has decided not simply to suffer the disadvantages of being so close to the United States. And the United States itself has realised the importance of trying to accommodate Mexico.

In the past there were huge attempts by the United States to prevent people from moving from Mexico *into* the United States; people seeking work, seeking jobs. So you had police, a border very well policed in order to prevent Mexicans who *seek*, who *look* for jobs, to *move* into the United States. The United States discovered that it was not working. It *can't* work.

There is a kind of economic osmosis where whatever you do, if you are rich, you are attractive to the poor. They will come, they'll even *risk* their own lives in order to come. So the United States tried very hard to prevent Mexicans going into the United States; they've given up, and the result was NAFTA. It is in the interest of the United States to try and create jobs in Mexico because, if you don't, the Mexicans will simply come, to the United States; so they're doing that.

Europe, Western Europe, is very wealthy. It has two Mexicos. One is Eastern Europe. If you want to prevent those Eastern Europeans to come to Western Europe, you jolly will have to create jobs in *Eastern* Europe, and Western Europe is actually *doing* that. They are *doing* that.

They'll help Eastern Europe to develop.

The whole of Western Europe will be doing it, the Germans are doing it.

The Germans basically started first of all with the East Germans but they are spending lots of money also helping the other countries of Eastern Europe to develop, including unfortunately, or *fortunately* for them, including Russia. Because they realise, Europeans realise including the Germans, if you don't help *Russia* to develop, one of these days you are going to be in trouble.

So it is in the interest of Western Europe, to help Eastern Europe including Russia. They are pouring a lot of money in that part of the world, in that part of Europe, to try and help it to develop.

I said Western Europe has two Mexicos. I have mentioned one. I'll jump the other. I jump Europe's second Mexico. I'll go to Asia. I'll go to Japan. Japan – a wealthy island, *very* wealthy indeed, but an *island*.

I don't think they're very keen on the unemployed of Asia to go to Japan. They'd rather help them where they are, and Japan is spending a lot of money in Asia, to help create jobs *in* Asia, prevent those Asians dreaming about going to Japan to look for jobs. In any case, Japan is too small, they can't find wealth there.

But apart from what Japan is doing, of course Asia *is* Asia; Asia has *China!* Asia has *India*, and the small countries of Asia are not very small. The population of Indonesia is twice the population of Nigeria, your biggest. So Asia is virtually in a category, of the Third World countries, of the Southern countries; Asia is almost in a category of its own. It is developing as a power, and Europe knows it, and the United States knows it. And in spite of the *huge* Atlantic, now they are talking about the Atlantic *Rim*. That is in recognition of the importance of Asia.

I go back to Europe. Europe has a second Mexico. And Europe's second Mexico is North Africa. North Africa is to Europe what Mexico is to the United States. North Africans who have no jobs will not go to Nigeria; they'll be thinking of Europe or the Middle East, because of the imperatives of geography and history and religion and language. North Africa is part of Europe and the Middle East.

Nasser was a great leader and a great *African* leader. I got on extremely well with him. Once he sent me a minister, and I had a long discussion with his minister at the State House here, and in the course of the discussion, the minister says to me, 'Mr. President, this is my first visit to Africa.'

North Africa, because of the pull of the Mediterranean, and I say, history and culture, and religion, North Africa is pulled towards the North. When North Africans look for jobs, they go to Western Europe and southern Western Europe, or they go to the Middle East. And Europe has a specific policy for North Africa, specific policy for North Africa. It's not only about development; it's also about security. Because of you don't do something about North Africa, they'll come.

Africa, south of the Sahara, is different; *totally* different. If you have no jobs here in Tanzania, where do you go? The Japanese have no fear that you people will flock to Japan. The North Americans have no fear that you people will flock to North America. Not even from West Africa. The Atlantic, the Atlantic as an ocean, like the Mediterranean, it has its own logic. But links North America and Western Europe, not North America and West Africa.

Africa south of the Sahara is isolated. That is the first point I want to make. South of the Sahara is totally isolated in terms of that configuration of developing power in the world in the 21st century – on its own. There is no centre of power in whose self-interest it's important to develop Africa, *no* centre. Not North America, not Japan, not Western Europe.

There's no self-interest to bother about Africa south of the Sahara. Africa south of the Sahara is on its own. *Na si jambo baya.* Those of you who don't know Kiswahili, I just whispered, 'Not necessarily bad.'

That's the first thing I wanted to say about Africa south of the Sahara. African leadership, the coming African leadership, will have to bear that in mind. You are on your own, Mr. Vice President.

You mentioned, you know, in the past, there was some Cold War competition in Africa and some Africans may have exploited it. I never did. I never succeeded in exploiting the Cold War in Africa. We suffered, we suffered through the Cold War.

Look at Africa south of the Sahara. I'll be talking about it later. Southern Africa, I mean, look at southern Africa; devastated because of the combination of the Cold War and apartheid. Devastated part of Africa. It could have been *very* different. But the Cold War is gone, thank God. But thank God the Cold War is gone, the chances of the Mobutus also is gone.

So that's the first thing I wanted to say about Africa south of the Sahara. Africa south of the Sahara in those terms is isolated. That is the point I said was not obvious and I had to explain it in terms in which I have tried to explain it.

The other one, the second point I want to raise is completely obvious. Africa has 53 nation-states, most of them in Africa south of the Sahara. If numbers were power, Africa would be the most powerful continent on earth. It is the weakest; so it's obvious numbers are not power.

So the second point about Africa, and again I am talking about Africa south of the Sahara; it is fragmented, fragmented. From the very beginning of independence 40 years ago, we were against that idea, that the continent is so fragmented. We called it the Balkanisation of Africa. Today, I think the Balkans are talking about the

Africanisation of Europe.

Africa's states are too many, too small, some make no logic, whether political logic or ethnic logic or anything. They are non-viable. It is not a confession....

Throw away all our ideas about socialism. Throw them away, give them to the Americans, give them to the Japanese, give them, so that they can, I don't know, they can do whatever they like with them. *Embrace* capitalism, fine! But you *have* to be self-reliant. You here in Tanzania don't dream that if you privatise every blessed thing, including the prison, then foreign investors will come rushing. No! No! Your are dreaming! *Hawaji!* They won't come! (*hawaji!*). You just try it. There is more to privatise in Eastern Europe than here.

Norman Manley, the Prime Minister of Jamaica, in those days the vogue was nationalisation, not privatisation. In those days the vogue was *nationalisation*. So Norman Manley was asked as Jamaica was moving towards independence: 'Mr. Prime Minister, are you going to nationalise the economy?' His answer was: 'You can't nationalise *nothing*.'

You people here are busy privatising not *nothing*, we did *build* something, we built *something* to privatise. But quite frankly, for the appetite of Europe, and the appetite of North America, this is privatising nothing.

The people with a really good appetite will go to Eastern Europe, they'll go to Russia, they'll not come rushing to Tanzania! Your blessed National Bank of Commerce, it's a branch of some major bank somewhere, and in Tanzania you say, 'It's so big we must divide it into pieces,' which is *nonsense*.

Africa south of the Sahara is isolated. Therefore, to develop, it will have to depend upon its own resources basically. Internal resources, nationally; and Africa will have to depend upon Africa.

The leadership of the future will have to devise, try to carry out policies of *maximum* national self-reliance and *maximum* collective self-reliance. They have no other choice. *Hamna!* (You don't have it!) And this, this need to organise collective self-reliance is what moves me to the second part.

The small countries in Africa must move towards either unity or co-operation, unity of Africa. The leadership of the future, of the 21st century, should have less respect, less respect for this thing called 'national sovereignty.' I'm not saying take up arms and destroy the state, no! This idea that we must *preserve* the Tanganyika, then *preserve* the Kenya as they *are*, is nonsensical!

The nation-states we in Africa, have inherited from Europe. They are the builders of the nation-states par excellence. For centuries they fought wars! The history of Europe, the history of the *building* of Europe is a history of war. And sometimes their wars when they get hotter although they're European wars, they call them *world wars*. And we all get involved. We fight even in Tanganyika here, we *fought* here, one world war.

These Europeans, powerful, where little Belgium is more powerful than the whole of Africa south of the Sahara put together; these *powerful* European states are moving towards unity, and you people are talking about the atavism of the tribe, this is nonsense! I am telling *you* people. How can anybody think of the tribe as the unity of the future? *Hakuna!* (There's nothing!).

Europe now, you can take it almost as God-given, Europe is not going to fight with Europe anymore. The Europeans are not going to take up arms against Europeans. They are moving towards unity – even the little, the little countries of the Balkans which are breaking up, Yugoslavia breaking up, but they are breaking up at the same time the building up is taking place. They break up and say we want to come into the *bigger* unity.

So there's a *building* movement, there's a *building* of Europe. These countries which have old, old sovereignties, countries of hundreds of years old; they are forgetting this, they are *moving* towards unity. And you people, you think Tanzania is sacred? What is Tanzania!

You *have* to move towards unity. If these powerful countries see that they have no future in the nation-states – *ninyi mnafikiri mna future katika nini*? (what future do you think you have?). So, if we can't *move*, if our leadership, our future leadership cannot move us to bigger nation-states, which I *hope* they are going to try; we tried and failed. I tried and failed. One of my biggest failures was actually that. I tried in East Africa and failed.

But don't give up because we, the first leadership, failed, no! *Unajaribu tena*! (You try again!). We failed, but the idea is a good idea. That these countries should come together.

Don't leave Rwanda and Burundi on their own. *Hawawezi kusurvive* (They cannot survive). They can't. They're locked up into a form of prejudice. If we can't move towards bigger nation-states, at least let's move towards greater co-operation. This is beginning to happen. And the new leadership in Africa should encourage it.

I want to say only one or two things about what is happening in southern Africa.

Please accept the logic of coming together. South Africa, small; South Africa is very small. Their per capita income now is, I think $2,000 a year or something around that. Compared with Tanzanians, of course, it is very big, but it's poor. If South Africa begins to tackle the problems of the legacy of apartheid, they have no money!

But compared with the rest of us, they are rich. And so, in southern Africa, there, there is also a kind of osmosis, also an economic osmosis. South Africa's neighbours send their job seekers *into* South Africa. And South Africa will simply have to accept the logic of that, that they are big, they are attractive. They attract the unemployed from Mozambique, and from Lesotho and from the rest. They have to accept that fact of life. It's a problem, but they have to accept it.

South Africa, and I am talking about post-apartheid South Africa. Post-apartheid South Africa has the most developed and the most dynamic private sector on the continent. It is white, so what? So forget it is white. It is South African, dynamic, highly developed. If the investors of South Africa begin a new form of trekking, you *have* to accept it.

It will be ridiculous, absolutely ridiculous, for Africans to go out seeking investment from North America, from Japan, from Europe, from Russia, and then, when these investors come from South Africa to invest in your own country, you say, 'a! a! These fellows now want to take over our economy' – this is nonsense. You can't have it both ways. You want foreign investors or you don't want foreign investors. Now, the most available foreign investors for you are those from South Africa.

And let me tell you, when Europe think in terms of investing, they *might* go to South Africa. When North America think in terms of investing, they *might* go to South Africa. Even Asia, if they want to invest, the first country they may think of in Africa *may* be South Africa. So, if *your* South Africa is going to be *your* engine of development, accept the reality, accept the reality. Don't accept this sovereignty, South Africa will reduce your sovereignty. What sovereignty do you have?

Many of these debt-ridden countries in Africa now have no sovereignty, they've lost it. *Imekwenda* (It's gone). *Iko mikononi mwa IMF na World Bank* (It's in the hands of the IMF and the World Bank). *Unafikiri kuna sovereignty gani*? (What kind of sovereignty do you think there is?)

So, southern Africa has an opportunity, southern Africa, the SADC group, *because* of South Africa.

Because South Africa now is no longer a destabiliser of the region, but a partner in development, southern Africa has a tremendous opportunity. But you need leadership, because if you get proper leadership there, within the next 10, 15 years, that region is going to be the ASEAN (Association of South-East Asian Nations) of Africa. And it is possible. But forget the protection of your sovereignties. I believe the South Africans will be sensitive enough to know that if they are not careful, there is going to be this resentment of big brother, but that big brother, frankly, is not very big.

West Africa. Another bloc is developing there, but that depends very much upon Nigeria my brother (looking at the Nigerian High Commissioner – Ambassador), very much so. Without Nigeria, the future of West Africa is a problem. West Africa is more balkanised than Eastern Africa. More balkanised, tiny little states.

The leadership will have to come from Nigeria. It came from Nigeria in Liberia; it has come from Nigeria in the case of Sierra Leone; it will have to come from Nigeria in galvanising ECOWAS.

But the military in Nigeria must allow the Nigerians to exercise that vitality in freedom. And it is my hope that they will do it.

I told you I was going to ramble and it was going to be messy, but thank you very much." – (Nyerere, in his speech at the University of Dar es Salaam, Tanzania, in G. Mwakikagile, *Nyerere and Africa: End of an Era*, op. cit., pp. 553 – 560)).

Globalisation is not going to solve our problems. It is controlled and dominated by the big powers, especially Western, including our former colonial masters, and is intended to benefit them.

We are now losing land and other natural resources everyday under globalisation as if we are still under colonial rule.

I have written about life under colonial rule – including racial injustices – in Tanganyika when I was growing up to show how life was during those days from the perspective of colonial subjects.

We hardly had any rights in our own country ruled and dominated by whites. We were just there – that was all – without any say. Our colonial rulers owned our countries. We were not even citizens of our own countries – were simply colonial subjects, and that is what we were called – British subjects – subjected to imperial domination by our British colonial masters.

Africans were lowest in the racial hierarchy, with Asians and Arabs ranked next to whites, partly to facilitate imperial rule but also because our rulers saw that as the natural order of things.

This brings up another point why I wrote this book and another one entitled *Life under British Colonial Rule: Recollections of an African.* I wanted to show how imperial rule profoundly affected the destiny of our people.

The impact colonial rulers had on us still reverberates today, manifested in many ways including the belief among some of our people that colonial rule was better than our traditional institutions of authority; that it had more advantages than disadvantages, and that the people who ruled us were superior to us – as if they had divine mandate to dominate us.

They are defending the indefensible. As Walter Rodney stated in his book, *How Europe Underdeveloped Africa*:

"The only positive development in colonialism was when it ended." – (Walter Rodney, *How Europe Underdeveloped Africa*, op. cit., p. 414).

Sadly, the liberation of Africa is not complete, especially in this era of globalisation dominated by Western powers, although China is also flexing her muscles in the international arena and has become a major player in Africa.

Although we are not completely free, we won something when colonial rule ended.

The first thing we got back when we won independence from our colonial rulers was dignity, what in Swahili we call *utu*. It is rooted not only in our humanity as equal human beings but also in what we are as a people with our own identity and history. It is rooted in our African-ness. As Nkrumah said:

"I am not African because I was born in Africa but because Africa was born in me."

Tragically, Pan-African solidarity, seeing ourselves as one in this era of globalisation, is virtually non-existent.

It is everyone for himself or herself. Even the people collectively constituting nations are for themselves, as individuals in their own countries, without caring about their collective wellbeing; a problem that has been compounded by bad leadership – responsible for economic mismanagement and political repression – which has caused "mass migration" from all parts of the continent as the people flee their countries in search of greener pastures and freedom in Europe, America and elsewhere round the globe.

Countries are also only for themselves. South Africans are for themselves. Kenyans are for themselves. Nigerians are for themselves. Tanzanians are for themselves. Ethiopians are for themselves; so are other Africans.

South Africans have even forgotten, or they simply ignore, all the assistance they were given and the sacrifices that were made by their brothers and sisters across the continent to support them during their darkest hour when they were fighting against apartheid.

They have, instead, expressed their gratitude to them in its crudest form by launching xenophobic attacks on fellow blacks from other African countries seeking employment and living in South Africa. Even the South African minister of foreign affairs, Naledi Pandor, described the attacks as Afrophobia when they were going on in 2019.

The attacks were nothing new. They started in 1994 soon after apartheid was formally abolished and the first black president in the nation's history, Nelson Mandela, assumed power; a fundamental change which encouraged other Africans from neighbouring countries and beyond to migrate to South Africa.

The influx triggered a violent response from black South Africans, especially those living in poverty-stricken townships who accused black foreigners of taking jobs away from them and "stealing" their women.

The attacks were carried out sometimes with the tacit approval of some South African officials – and even outright encouragement – while the national government itself looked the other way, remained silent, or expressed mild condemnation of the violence against black immigrants.

The Pan-African solidarity we had during the struggle for independence in the sixties and seventies, when we supported each other in our quest for freedom from colonial rule, is ancient history.

It is as if we had such solidarity only because we were fighting for independence and, after most of our countries attained sovereign status, because we were united in the struggle against white minority rule in the countries of southern Africa and Portuguese Guinea/Cape Verde in West Africa.

That is no longer the case today even when our survival is threatened and when we are being ruthlessly exploited by major powers in this era of globalisation which many of our leaders and the elite see as a blessing to us, as they reap for themselves the fruits of imperial "benevolence."

We no longer act as one people to preserve, protect and promote our interests as Africans in a world that does *not* care about us – except our resources. And it shouldn't, if we don't care about ourselves as much as we should and work together as one people.

It will take a lot of pride in what we are as a people and in seeing Africa as one for us to move forward.

Part Two:

Colonial Mentality
and the Destiny of Africa

COLONIAL MENTALITY among many Africans including leaders has played a critical role in determining the fate of African countries since independence. And it continues to play the same role in shaping the destiny of our continent.

As I have stated before, when we were conquered by Europeans, we were also conquered by ideas. They were European ideas. They were not spread by bullets and they still dominate the minds of many Africans.

Colonial mentality fosters feelings of inferiority and insecurity which, in the minds of those who are mentally colonised, can be overcome only by emulating our former colonial masters in every conceivable way.

Even the worst vices of our former colonial rulers, exemplified by the moral depravity of their Western life styles, become virtues to those who have colonial mentality. Thus, they end up debasing themselves just because they want to be like our former colonial rulers, especially in terms of thinking and life styles.

They don't want to think for themselves. They don't even want to help themselves.

One of the most tragic results of having colonial

mentality is perpetual dependency on our former colonial masters. This dependency has extended to other powers, mostly European, and even to some of our fellow Third Worlders, especially the Chinese.

It is as if we cannot do anything for ourselves. We have to depend on other people to do things for us, including erecting and paying for buildings we ourselves could have built and paid for.

The most embarrassing and humiliating example – ruthlessly public and in the international spotlight – is the headquarters of the African Union (AU) built and paid for by the Chinese from the People's Republic of China as a "gift" to us; even the Taiwanese would have done that had we begged them to do so.

The African Union itself as a continental institution in pursuit of unity and solidarity is even patterned after the European Union without the slightest attempt by our leaders to give it a distinctive identity – of its own as an African entity without being a carbon copy of an institution outside Africa whose members couldn't care less if we didn't exist anymore.

It is even "named" after the European Union. Just look at the names. Europeans have the "European Union,." So, we are going to have the "African Union." They also call it "the EU." We call ours "the AU" – instead of giving it a distinctive appellation.

They have "the Euro," as their currency, so ours is going to be "the Afro."

The list goes on and on.

Even in the sixties, Africa's decade of independence more than any other because the largest number of our countries emerged from colonial rule during that period, our leaders were no more imaginative than the current ones are.

Back then, during those halcyon days when we were enveloped in euphoria of a blissful decade of rising expectations, our leaders gleefully talked about forming a

"United States of Africa" – in other words a USA. Why not? Americans had a USA – so we also had to have a USA, and with almost exactly the same name.

We had to follow in the footsteps of the United States of America pursuing our dream of a united Africa. That is why our leaders called our prospective union a "United States of Africa." Unfortunately, it remained an elusive dream decades later when we couldn't even build the headquarters of the African Union and had to wait for the Chinese to do that for us.

There are many other examples in all African countries, only less glaring than the African Union headquarters, which demonstrate out inability and unwillingness to help ourselves as we wait for foreigners to come and do whatever we ask them to do for us as if we are a continent of infants.

Another shameful example of Africa's inability – mainly unwillingness and even plain refusal – to help herself has to do with the proposed East African federation.

There are six member states of the East African Community (EAC) which are trying to form a federation. They are Kenya, Uganda and Tanzania – the original members of this regional bloc – together with newly admitted Rwanda, Burundi, and South Sudan.

Yet they say they don't have the money even for drafting a constitution of the proposed federation – funds needed to defray expenses incurred in pursuing the constitutional process including conducting opinion surveys across the region to find out how the people feel about uniting their countries under one government and what kind of union they should have if they agree to have one at all. The federation is intended to be a people-centred union, not one agreed upon only by the leaders.

The money is also needed to meet expenses incurred by the members of the exploratory committee or committees including those who are going to draft the constitution.

But there is no money for them to do the job. It is going to cost $4.8 million.

Yet all these countries combined can easily contribute some money and have a fund of $4.8 million needed to facilitate the constitutional process of working on a constitution for the proposed federation they want to form for their own collective wellbeing, security and prosperity. Still, they say they don't have the money – they can't afford it.

Who is going to believe them or take them seriously that they really want to unite? Just one country alone can afford that amount.

So, what are they going to do? Are they going to beg the very same people they say they want to break away from and be truly independent to help us unite?

If they do, it will be very humiliating to beg them to give us $4.8 million to help pay for the constitutional process – may be even for political integration itself which will cost even more – in pursuit of the elusive dream of achieving genuine independence from our former colonial masters and even new ones.

According to a report, "EAC Seeks $4.8m for Political Union Project," in *The Citizen*, Dar es Salaam, Tanzania, 23 November 2019:

"The East African Community (EAC) requires $4.8 million to accomplish its Political Federation project.

The secretariat is urging for a special funding arrangement to undertake and complete the process in time.

'It is an expensive project requiring substantial financial investment,' said the secretary general Liberat Mfumukeko.

He admitted when speaking in Kampala last week that the process was behind schedule due to scarcity of funds.

'In our estimation, the process of drafting the Constitution will require resources to the tune of $ 4.8

million,' he said.

Ambassador Mfumukeko was speaking in the Uganda capital during the launching of the National Stakeholders Consultations to Draft the EAC Political Confederation.

He added that the consultations would ensure full participation of the EAC citizens in the desired integration process.

According to him, the development of the constitution of the proposed EAC Confederation was 'a political process that requires high level of inclusion.'

The drafting of the EAC Political Confederation is being undertaken by a team of constitutional experts nominated by the six partner states.

The 18-member team is chaired by Justice Dr. Benjamin Odoki, the Chief Justice Emeritus of Uganda and the process was projected to be completed in 2022 with its adoption by the [heads of state] summit.

Launching the consultations, President Yoweri Museveni of Uganda said the envisaged East African Political Federation will bring prosperity to the region.

'It will bring prosperity which can be attained through trade and economic growth,' he said at his Entebbe State House on Monday.

He added that the envisaged political union would also guarantee strategic security for smaller member countries of the Community from external threats.

He said the political confederation he launched was 'a transitional model' to political federation.

Speaking at the event, the Chairperson of the Team of Constitutional Experts Justice, Dr. Odoki, said the team has been to various parts of the world studying the confederation systems.

He added that they have also finalized a study and analysing the EAC establishment in order to align it with the practice of confederations.

Political federation is the ultimate goal of the EAC regional integration project and the fourth after the

Customs Union, Common Market, and Monetary Union.

The process has, nonetheless, been slow. In 2017, the Summit of the Heads of State agreed on political confederation as a model for political federation.

A team tasked to develop the draft constitution was to present its report to the regional leaders during their ordinary summit on November 30[th.]

However, the summit which was to take place in Arusha has been postponed indefinitely." – ("EAC Seeks $4.8m for Political Union Project," *The Citizen*, Dar es Salaam, Tanzania, 23 November 2019).

It is really a shame that the six member states of the EAC which are contemplating forming a political federation have exposed themselves to such ridicule and contempt, claiming they can't afford $4.8 million to fund the constitutional process.

They just don't want to pay for it.

We always – at least most of the time – beg other people, and plead with them, to help us even for small amounts of money we desperately need to pursue unity – in East Africa in this case; a union that is supposed to help our countries achieve true independence.

But that is nothing new. In all parts of Africa, it is common for us to wait for our saviours from outside the continent to help us in almost all areas of life, including digging wells to get some water; sometimes even to build latrines.

This chronic dependency on the paternalistic benevolence of our former colonial masters and others, which is a product of colonial mentality and lack of self-confidence and self-respect, has emasculated us as the rest of the world laughs at us – for one simple reason:

There is no other continent where the people are so dependent on others outside their continent; not even some of the poorest in Asia and Latin America.

We don't even have middle-income countries, not even

a handful, the way Asians and Latin Americans do.

The largest number of the poorest countries in the world are African. The least developed countries in the world are also African.

There is no question that colonialism played a major role in the underdevelopment of Africa. But we *cannot*, more than half a century after we won independence, continue to blame colonialism and our former colonial rulers for everything that has gone wrong – and that still goes wrong – in Africa.

There is all this talk about an African renaissance. Yet nothing concrete has been done to achieve the goal besides making speeches and writing papers about it. And when we try to do something, we always follow in the footsteps of others.

Where is our genius and ingenuity we have always been so proud of as the mother of civilisation and the origin of mankind? Are we lying to ourselves and to the rest of the world? Are we unable to do for ourselves what other people do for themselves?

The genius of a people lies within and does not need external stimuli to be awakened even if it is in a deep slumber.

We have even failed to project, promote and defend the African personality in the international arena where we are despised more than anybody else because of what we are as a people, also because we have failed to live to our full potential and do for ourselves what other people – even those on the same level with us – are able to do for themselves.

The people themselves, individually and collectively, are responsible for this illness. That is what colonial mentality is. It is a mental illness.

Millions of our people are afflicted with this mental illness. But there is no question that the elite have played an even bigger role in perpetuating this disease, fostering colonial mentality as if it were a blessing to us.

Educated in the Western intellectual tradition – even in our schools, not just in the West, since our schools are a product of Western colonial educational systems – and in other non-African countries, members of the elite who collectively constitute the leadership in our countries are so proud of their Western education and their intellectual preparation in other academic institutions outside Africa that they have severed ties with the societies – mostly of traditional Africa – which produced them and have become detached from the masses whom they are supposed to lead. All that is a manifestation of colonial mentality and its debilitating effects on the African personality.

They are irrelevant to Africa and even dangerous to Africa's well-being when they continue to insulate themselves from the societies which produced and nurtured them and when they see themselves as an extension of Europe and America and their leadership positions as no more than a source of income and power to advance their own interests at the expense of their fellow countrymen and women.

Yet they took the reins of power when we attained sovereign status after the end of colonial rule, and others through the years have assumed positions of authority, vowing to free our continent from all forms of imperial domination and exploitation – political, economic, social, cultural, intellectual and even spiritual – only to capitulate and even bow in servile submission to the very forces they vowed to fight against. As Professor Messay Kebede, an Ethiopian, states in his book, *Africa's Quest for a Philosophy of Decolonization*:

"The saviors of Africa turned out to be its plunderers and a complete disillusionment took hold of Africans. Economic crises, perpetual political instability, and social tensions, together with rampant corruption and nepotism, became the defining features of Africa.

If anything, the depravity and predatory nature of the postcolonial elite testify to the complete loss of its sense of accountability to society.

One explanation is uprootedness: because uprootedness dilutes respect and commitment, it takes away the sense of obligation to the people from the political elite.

When perceived as essentially inadequate, society is likened to a raw material that must be fashioned at will, it inspires no obligation to its demiurges. As a result of ceasing to belong to the native society on account of its Western education, the intelligentsia panders to patronization whose conspicuous result is the collapse of all ethical relationship with the social community.

To summarize, the elitist attitude echoes the colonial mentality means that the moral bankruptcy of the educated elite is a direct consequence of the endorsement of the idea of primitive Africa." – (Messay Kebede, *Africa's Quest for a Philosophy of Decolonization*, Amsterdam, New York, NY: Rodopi B.V., 2004, p. 162).

Professor Kebede goes on to state:

"The act by which Africans welcome Western education is the act by which they acquiesce to the colonial discourse on Africa: the one is inseparable from the other. As a result, educated Africans are unable to adopt a moral standard: the contempt – mostly unconscious – that they feel for Africanness totally deprives them of ethical relationships with themselves and their original society. Disdain and non-accountability appear to them as the only way by which they demonstrate their complete emancipation from their legacy.

Imperative, therefore, is the recognition as a major explanation of African numerous impediments the fact that modern African states have simply replaced the colonial states. Because 'Africans replaced the European officials right to the top of the bureaucracy' without the prior dismantling of the colonial state and methods, especially without a far-reaching decolonization of the educated and political elites, small wonder the same structure and turn of mind usher in similar results." – (Ibid.).

He further states:

"The rehabilitation of African traditions suggests an orientation that should ward off elitism: instead of imposing the imitation of an external model, the thinking should be committed to building modernity on African realities and centrality.
Most ethnophilosophers, such as Léopold Sédar Senghor, Kwame Nkrumah, and Julius Nyerere, refer the future of Africa to the idea of African socialism. The reference implies the inadequacy of the Western model; it also pledges to rehabilitate 'the traditional social order and to seek salvation in the pristine values of our [African] ancestors.'
Since the Western model is inadequate, Africans must return to their source. This return is all the more necessary as the search for authenticity provides a solution to African failure.
The delay of modernization suggests that the path to socialist development alone is suitable for African personality. Above all, the revival of tradition and the reconnection of Africans with the idea of a free precolonial Africa are perceived as the best way to decolonize the African mind. Decolonization is impossible so long as Africans do not rediscover and reconcile themselves with the idea of a free Africa." – (Ibid., pp. 162 – 163).

A return to roots and to the past is vital to Africa's well-being, future and integrity and even her sanity.
Tragically, many African don't like their heritage – they don't even like their physical features including complexion and hair texture.

Skin bleaching is common among a very large number of them; so is preference for straight hair including wigs made of hair imported from Asia.

The less African they are in terms of appearance, the better it is for them. They assume a new "identity." They believe in deluding themselves. They have lost their mind – "the mind of Africa," to use Dr. Willie Abraham's expression which is also the title of his highly acclaimed philosophical work, *The Mind of Africa*.

Many Africans hate themselves. You can't say you don't hate yourself when you are trying to be what you are not. There are even those who not only don't want to look African – they don't even want to sound African. They are so brainwashed that they are ashamed of their African accents. They want to sound British, French, American, and so on.

All that is a result of having colonial mentality which has many Africans believing that almost anything that is non-African is better than everything that is African, with things European and American being the best.

Even our food is "bad." If it is European or Asian, it is better than ours.

White people are, of course, on top of the racial hierarchy. It is a reality that is acknowledged even in a subservient way by some Africans who literally worship whites.

Samira Sawlani recorded her observations of this disturbing phenomenon in her article, "Tourism, White Privilege and Colonial Mentality in East Africa," in *Pambazuka News*:

"White persons are revered in East Africa. Local black people go to ridiculous lengths to please whites, thereby promoting the baseless concept of white supremacy. It is a practice deeply rooted in colonialism.

We walked into the police station in Uganda. My white

British friend who wanted to file a complaint had asked me to accompany her. The three officers behind the desk stood up immediately, one giving her his chair, the other rushing to take notes and the third, with a great deal of concern on his face asked her what had happened.

Sat in the waiting area were a pregnant woman and an elderly gentleman, both were black Ugandans. The lady had been waiting over two hours for the police to attend to her while the gentleman had spoken to them regarding his issue and been told to wait. He'd been waiting for almost three hours. My friend on the other hand was dealt with immediately and within thirty minutes all procedures had been carried out and her complaint both logged and addressed.

Two years prior to this I was stood in a queue at a bank in Uganda, ahead of me was a white gentleman and in front of him was an elderly Ugandan lady. The Bank Manager came out and bypassed the lady at the front and made a beeline to the white man. I stood, absolutely baffled by both her actions and the collective silence of everyone in the bank as if this was a normal occurrence. As I called out to the manager and pointed out that the Ugandan lady was first, she ignored me and continued on with her tasks.

This was to be the first of many situations I witnessed of what I believe can be defined as 'white privilege' in East Africa, a right earned through the continued domination of white supremacy.

Two weeks ago the media reported that the Kenyan Government have offered a free holiday to the family of a 15 year old American tourist who was 'harassed by a police officer' because he mistook her for terror suspect Samantha Lewthwaite. If it was a Somali family holidaying in Kenya and their son had been mistaken for Abu Ubaidah the new leader of Al-Shabaab would the same courtesy have been offered? I highly doubt it.

Why is this? Because the American tourist was white

and thus she along with numerous others enjoy a certain privilege earned by the colour of her skin.

The concept of white privilege is associated with predominantly white societies such as the United States of America and Great Britain. In these parts of the world it manifests in a variety of ways, from being as simple as wanting to buy a pair of 'nude shoes' and finding that 'nude' in the fashion industry equates to that which matches white skin, to forming the foundation of a society where young black men like Trayvon Martin and Michael Brown can be killed based upon appearance and justice to their loved ones denied.

These examples may not always apply to countries like Kenya and Uganda where the population is predominantly black. However borne in this part of the world are types of phenomena which fall into this category, particularly as they often create some form of disadvantage for the local population.

Like the example of the bank mentioned above, it is in shops, restaurants, bars and other social spaces where white privilege often instigated by people of colour can be seen.

Almost every person in Kenya that I interviewed cited the example of how security guards at shopping centres will often not frisk or search through the belongings of white mall goers yet non-white visitors are always subject to a thorough check. Is this in itself not reinforcing the view that white people cannot be involved in criminal activity or terror and are therefore exempt from the process?

This difference in attitude and perception adds to the dehumanising narrative, which has for centuries formed the basis of how black people have been viewed. This stance which assumes the black individual is inherently prone to partake in crime is then juxtaposed with the inherent civility and innocence associated with the white population.

In Uganda 29-year-old lawyer Lisa Mbabazi complains about staff at food courts, restaurants and bars choosing to serve white customers first, leaving people like her feeling like a second class citizen. In her opinion this practice upholds a system inherited from colonialism which 'characterises black people as being inferior and thus not worthy of the same level of services and rights enjoyed by their white counterparts.'

A waitress in Kampala argued against this accusation telling me 'It is just us being hospitable to our foreign guests.' I challenged her on this asking if the same treatment was given to black tourists from other parts of Africa or visitors from Asia and her response was a baffled silence.

Nationality may bring some form of privileges however it comes second to race. A friend who is a Black British passport holder and her two children were stood in the immigration queue at Julius Nyerere International Airport, Tanzania. As she stepped forward to the counter she was stopped as the immigration officer pointed to the white couple behind her to come forward first. This illustrated that ultimately 'passport privilege' is beaten by that which is earned through skin colour.

A bar owner in Nairobi states that his reasoning for prioritising white guests is because they tip better and spend more than their black counterparts. He argued that white people in East Africa enjoy a certain level of privilege because they as foreigners or descendants of foreigners are considered to have money which provides them with multiple benefits as a result of race and wealth. Thus leading me to conclude that the benefits gained by the white population be they expats, tourists or residents is a result of the way they are perceived, a concept inherited from our colonial past.

The continued dominance of white superiority in this part of the world or indeed other former colonies such as India and Pakistan is not only evident in the treatment of the white population but also in the covert and overt ways in which we aspire to replicate and meet standards of the white western world. We want our buildings and cities to look like New York and London, a branch of Kentucky Fried Chicken opens in Kampala and it becomes cause for celebration despite the fact that local chicken and chips shops have been around for decades.

Similarly eurocentric ideals of beauty, foreign products and all that is approved by those Western countries where a white population is dominant, continue to be held in high esteem. As said by a Ugandan branding expert 'We love Japanese electronics, however this is also due to the fact that these brands have obtained Western approval.'

In her novel, *Looking for Transwonderland*, Noo Saro Wiwa speaks to a young Nigerian student who tells her 'People don't want to read books by Nigerians living in Nigeria. If Kaine Agary had published 'yellow-yellow' in the US, Nigerians would have taken an interest in it.' This is largely because of the power of Western validation which has also resulted in not enough value being given by society to local products, services and talent.

In an interview, Nigerian musician Femi Kuti said: 'An African will prefer to be called John-Philip. If you said your name was Chukwu Emeka Afongkudong they will say you are from the village. You are backward. How can you have such a name? We really look down on our culture and heritage instead of being proud of it.'

The elite in East Africa often choose to travel to Europe or America for healthcare services. For example, in 2003, President Museveni of Uganda spent thousands of pounds to fly his daughter to Germany where she gave birth. 2013 World Bank figures show the infant mortality rate (no. of infants dying before the age of 1) per 1000 live births stood at 3 in Germany while in the same year the figure was 44 in Uganda. Though President Museveni cited 'security reasons' for his decision, we see once again that for the rich and the famous only healthcare facilities in the white western world will do.

The greatest irony in this matter is the fact that in recent times leaders in both Kenya and Uganda have partaken in Anti-Western rhetoric and gained much support from the populace for this.

In Kenya, where both the President and Deputy President are facing trial at the International Criminal Court many have called for the case to be terminated and accused the ICC of being racist and a puppet of the West. While in Uganda strong support for the Anti-Homosexuality law was seen as making a statement to Europe and America.

So why over 50 years after decolonisation does white supremacy and white privilege continue to manifest in East Africa? Why are phrases such as 'African timing' or 'African standards' used in a derogatory fashion?

Some would choose to take a historical perspective on this, and quote the likes of theorists such as Frantz Fanon and Albert Memmi for who 'a salient effect of colonization is the internalization of the inferior perception that is imposed on him/her by the colonizer.' *In Black Skin, White Masks*, Fanon writes, 'If there is an inferiority complex, it is the outcome of a double process; – primarily, economic; – subsequently, the internalization – or, better, the epidermalization – of this inferiority.'

These incidents, that way of thinking, that perception many possess fall under the heading of 'colonial mentality' which Kwame Gyekye describes: 'Colonial rule infects the subjected people with a certain mental outlook, a certain pattern of thinking. This pattern of thinking has come to be dubbed "colonial mentality" and to be regarded as a negative intellectual attribute…. resulting in the tendency to regard foreign cultural products as of much greater worth than those of the indigenous culture.' (Gyekye 1997:234)

If we are to go with this school of thought then the argument is that part of the hangover from colonialism is the belief both enforced and internalised that white people and culture continue to hold some form of superiority. In her paper, 'Skin Bleaching, Self Hatred and Colonial Mentality,' Dr Yaba Blay attributes part of the responsibility for this to the media and society as a whole 'to have light skin means that you may have White (or other) ancestry. And if in this context, Whiteness has been historically projected as inherently better than Blackness, to have White blood automatically renders one better than average. While at the surface level, this type of thinking can absolutely be plugged into the "colonial mentality" definition, we cannot treat skin bleachers as if they exist within an ahistoric, apolitical vacuum. They are members of a larger society that has, and continues to privilege Whiteness.'

And so we frequently witness and experience in parts of East Africa, as in many other parts of the world, this internalised colonial mentality which crossed from an appreciation of all that is white and western to becoming an aspiration, a standard on and by which judgements are made.

The colonialists were known to oppress their subjects and in exercising this mentality we ourselves give birth to an internalised oppression, one which many do not even realise they are partaking in." – (Samira Sawlani, "Tourism, White Privilege and Colonial Mentality in East Africa," *Pambazuka News*, 22 October 2014).

Yet the people many Africans glorify so much are some of the very same people who despise us, so much so that they don't even see black people as full human beings; they consider blacks to be subhuman at best.

This mentality has even extended to Africans themselves.

One good example is South Africa where this malady afflicts blacks probably more than any other people on the continent because of the way they suffered under apartheid. Many of them have internalised the mentality of their oppressors and, unconsciously, even think like them.

These are the people who suffered extreme racial oppression and degredation under one of the most brutal regimes in African colonial and post-colonial history. Yet they have adopted attitudes of their their oppressors towards fellow Africans. There are other cases on the continent but South Africa's is extreme in that regard.

Black South Africans identify with their former oppressors who felt superior to them. Now they also feel superior to fellow Africans.

It is a form of colonial mentality many black South Africans have. They have even gone on the rampage attacking fellow blacks from other African countries to cleanse their country of the black "scourge" that is destroying and tarnishing the image of their beautiful country which they think is not even African – because their white oppressors transformed it into another part of the white world. And black South Africans are proud of that, distancing themselves from fellow blacks in other parts of the continent.

Some of them don't even consider themselves to be Africans because true Africans are those in countries such as Congo, Burundi, Burkina Faso, Malawi, Mozambique, Tanzania, Benin, Sierra Leone, Mali, Senegal, Chad, South Sudan where extreme poverty is endemic, diseases rampant, security unheard of, since the police are virtually nonexistent, and where there are no schools – let alone desks in classrooms – and where children are taught under trees unlike in civilised and westernised South Africa.

Black South Africans don't even appreciate the vital role their African brothers and sisters played in helping to free them from brutal oppression under apartheid.

One Nigerian scholar, Said Adejumobi, who lived and taught in South Africa and later became a professor observed this tragic and disturbing phenomenon and stated the following on what he witnessed in a country which prides itself of being the rainbow nation in the post-apartheid era in an article aptly entitled, "Shame on South Africa!: Black South Africans are Suffering from Colonial Mentality":

"I lived in South Africa for two years. I was a research and post-doctoral fellow at the University of Cape Town. I was fortunate to be in South Africa at that moment and also in that university. This is because that was a period in which there was an intellectual battle over the soul and direction of the South African project through the nature of knowledge production and consumption.

The University of Cape Town is an excellent university with the best knowledge infrastructure on the continent. But the university at that point was the hotbed of the struggle to restructure knowledge production in South Africa. Mahmood Mamdani, a Uganda scholar – now at Columbia University – led the struggle to change the curriculum on Africa in the university from apartheid-based to a post-apartheid Africa focused one. Mamdani's close allies and associates including the late C.S.L Chachage, a professor of sociology from Tanzania joined the fray in the battle.

But we lost the battle; South Africa was unprepared for change. In the absence of change, apartheid will assume another form and shape; black on black violence will deepen; and the psychology of domination will recreate itself. This is the whole talk about xenophobia in South Africa.

For any discerning mind, what is happening now in South Africa is predictable. I saw it coming, and I left South Africa when I did. I recall informing my students, 'South Africa is a country on the edge; it may implode from within.' Without reshaping the curriculum on Africa; without decolonising the minds of the people; without owning up and admitting the historical role played by other African countries in South Africa's liberation struggle, South Africans rarely know who they are and where they are coming from.

Beyond mere cliches of the leadership of the African National Congress (ANC), and some cadres in the South African liberation movement, majority of South Africans especially the blacks do not see themselves as Africans.

When they comment on Africa, they refer to 'you people from Africa.' The mindset created under apartheid is that Africa is a jungle, where people are beasts, hungry and hopeless. The mindset remains unchanged and South Africans especially blacks don't want to identify with this. Coming from a history of denial and deprivation, South African blacks don't want to associate with those who have a semblance of their perceived former image; those who are deprived and hopeless.

They therefore see themselves differently, and far better than other Africans. They often tend to compare themselves with Europeans and Americans, with little or no African identity. This is the basis of the resentment, which they now call xenophobia.

Winnie Mandela is right when she laid the blame of the attack on fellow blacks from other African countries on the doorstep of the government given its failure to deliver on the long promises of political liberation; but this is only one part of the story, not the full story. Poverty and affluence live side by side in South Africa. Cape Town is one of the most beautiful cities in the World that I have ever seen. What I call 'Mainland' Cape Town is far better than the city of Paris or London. But that is how far it goes.

On the other side of 'mainland' Cape Town is 'cape town the ghetto' – these are the townships. 'Cape Town the ghetto' is worse than any slum I have ever seen in my life. I saw about five families all with children living in a single room. People sleep under the bed, in the corridor, kitchen etc. It is the most wicked and inhuman condition any human soul can live in. It is worse than Mushin, Ajegunle or any other slum in Lagos, Nigeria.

Political liberation has done nothing to change their lives.

The media manipulation in South Africa is to heap the blame of the condition of the poor South African blacks on foreigners mainly blacks from other African countries. They are depicted as job snatchers, criminals, drug pushers, crooks, etc. They are basically criminalised. Every non-South African black is seen as a job migrant, who has come to deny job to a Black South African.

The stage was set for a conflagration. There were cases in which people were thrown off the moving train and killed. The media and the government call it xenophobia; but I call criminality. Criminality was tolerated and inadvertently promoted to deflect the condition of the country, and explain off its inadequacies.

Mahmood Mamdani was fond of saying that South Africa is a poor country. Many South Africans detest it. His argument is that there is a tiny minority that is very rich, and affluent, while the majority of the people live in abject poverty unparallelled in any other African country. If the wealth of the nation is aggregated, their living standard will fall, and South Africa may not be better than many other African countries. The result of the warning signal being flagged by Mamdani is what is unfolding in South Africa today.

The structural dimension to the attack on people from other African countries by South African blacks is in two directions. First, the knowledge system is trapped in the legacies of apartheid, and as such black South Africans hardly appreciate the richness of African history and culture, hence the need to have changed mindset towards their fellow Africans.

The immediate step every African country took after decolonisation was to reshape the curriculum and rewrite their history. This in some cases involved importing scholars from other African countries to assist in the project. This was never to happen in South Africa. The effect is that the apartheid social construction of Africa and black identity is what still resonates in the minds of many South African blacks.

Unfortunately, people who volunteered to help South Africa achieve transformation in the educational sector never got the kind of political support needed from the South African political leadership including the ANC.

The second structural dimension to the attack on fellow black Africans is the orgy of self-denial which South Africa's political leadership and the ANC are engaged in. Hardly is the correct story of the liberation struggle told publicly to South African citizens. What is often told is a story of self-victory. The role played by other African countries is hardly mentioned and South African middle class elite (including the media) are fond of saying, 'we do not owe other African countries anything.' Of course, they do.

I recall that when Julius Nyerere died (I was in South Africa then), he was depicted in the media in a very negative sense. Headlines like the 'tyrant is gone' replete media stories on him. This is highly unfortunate. Julius Nyerere was one of the most steadfast leaders on South Africa's liberation struggle – committed his country's scarce resources, diplomatic strength and military support for the ANC. Nyerere was not to be celebrated but vilified. This is one of the gains of self-denial.

Nigeria was one of the frontline states and participated actively in South Africa's liberation struggle. Our resources, foreign policy, diplomatic strength and entire citizens commitment were put behind our South African brothers and sisters. I recall as a university undergraduate, I contributed money and participated in anti-apartheid campus movements. Our soul was with our South African brethren, is this our reward for supporting South Africa's liberation?

Today, South Africa is benefiting more than any other

African country in the African integration project. South African companies, like MTN are abroad in many African countries making super profit, but South Africans are attacking the citizens of those countries in South Africa.

There is no recorded case of either a South African citizen or company being maltreated in any other African country. South Africa must of necessity reciprocate the gesture and good will of other African countries, even if it chooses to tell the story of the anti-apartheid struggle differently.

The South African government must act and act fast in ensuring that other African citizens are not molested and attacked in South Africa.

The current attacks are definitely unacceptable and condemnable. Mbeki's African renaissance should not be about his people killing other African citizens; Pan-Africanism will not stand in the face of the current onslaught on other Africans. Mbeki, Zuma and other leaders of the ANC must act, and act fast!" – (Said Adejumobi, "Shame on South Africa!: Black South Africans are Suffering from Colonial Mentality," *The New Black Magazine*, 28 May 2008, and in *The Guardian*).

Yet the very same people black South Africans so desperately want to identify with – white people in Europe and America – don't care about them anymore than they do about other blacks on the continent. Many whites – not all – see them as just "monkeys" like the rest of their brethren in other African countries. There are even some whites who feel sorry for them for being so brainwashed.

They are trying to run away from themselves but they can't. They are stuck with their black African identity and that infuriates them. Whites will never accept them as equals; some of them do, but the majority won't. And the majority rules.

Even our status as sovereign nations, decades after the end of colonial rule, means absolutely nothing to our former colonial rulers. They still think they own our countries – and us as well; we are no more than servile servants to them or should, at the very least, be that.

Here is another example of colonial mentality from the first black African country to emerge from colonial rule. As Sylvanus Akorsu stated in his article, "Ghana, the Country That Hates Its Citizens," *Modern Ghana*:

"I have not travelled the world but I know every country loves its citizens and gives them priority when it comes to the distribution of public goods and services. The only country I know that doesn't follow this rule is Ghana.

We have this unproductive façade of a cliché called Ghanaian hospitality, something we use to disadvantage citizens. I do not say foreigners should be ignored but when you chose to love your guest more than yourself, then it is an anomaly....

The hatred for the Ghanaian permeates almost every aspect of our society but when it is perpetrated by public office holders who have been appointed and placed as stewards over our resources, and then it becomes more painful.

Take a good look at our tax administration. Almost every foreigner who comes here to do business of any kind is given tax exemption, because the person is bringing foreign exchange. According to Dr. Charles Ackah, a Senior Research Fellow of Institute of Social, Statistical and Economic Research (ISSER), University of Ghana, annual tax exemption for companies doing Foreign Direct Investments (FDI) in Ghana amounts to 4billion Cedis. This includes mining companies and free zone companies.

Over the years, these companies repatriated their profits to their countries of origin and that often leaves our cedi vulnerable. Our laws say they must retain some of their earnings here but they don't and repatriate everything with impunity.

I recently went to Osu in Accra to buy some office

equipment for my office and stepped into a huge office Mart belonging to Lebanese, packed with customers. After taking their proforma invoice, they attached a tax exemption form to it so that we will not take withholding tax from the amount when issuing them a cheque.

I moved 150 meters down into another shop owned by a Ghanaian, smaller than the Lebanese one and realized their prices were a little higher for some of the equipment as compared to the earlier shop but at the same time, a majority of the items were the same or even cheaper. When I inquired whether they had tax exemption, they responded in the negative with the explanation that they applied but were turned down.

Let a young Ghanaian start a small business today; the next day, GRA staff will be there to harass him for a pittance.

We tax everybody called Ghanaian including the pure water seller, head porter and single parents with 'apampam' or table top retail. Talk to the few daring young men and women who were brave enough to start as entrepreneurs and they will tell you their headache is tax. Is it wrong to give the Ghanaian tax holiday so that he can build his business and employ more Ghanaians?

I read that the petroleum agreement signed between Ghana and AKER Energy, the finance ministry granted up to $800million dollars tax exemption to the company; this includes all importations into the country.

Two months ago I was window shopping on Alibaba and saw a nice but moderately priced bed sheet and decided to try my visa card, because I have never used it to buy online before. When the item arrived, I paid import duty on it! Just one lousy poor man's bedsheet ooh.

So why do we leave the big money and keep chasing the small ones and be crying all the time that domestic revenue is low?

If you go looking for accommodation and you are a Ghanaian, you are most likely to be denied if a foreigner comes seeking the same apartment.

Our police are friendly to foreigners, especially the Europeans and Americans.

It's as if you commit a crime by being a Ghanaian in your own country.

We are ready to pay foreigners four times what we are ready to pay a Ghanaian for the same job! This is very prevalent in our sports, particularly football.

If you have a case with a foreigner and you reported it to the police, you will become complainant turned accused!

What is wrong with us? Is it inferiority complex or what? Why do we hate ourselves?

We allow foreigners to break our laws with glee and we are often spineless in taking action against them.

Aisha Huang and 'Aisha Rosewood' are fresh on our minds, when our Attorney General filed a *nolle prosequi* and she was later deported. Yet Ghanaians with minor mining infractions are quickly prosecuted and jailed! We are that wicked!

I remember how the then Tourism and Diaspora Relations Minister Hon. Asamoah Boateng caused the dismissal of a director of immigration, Hodari Okine for applying the immigration law against an Italian who entered the country with fake documents and was therefore asked to return on the same flight he came on. The Italian happened to have an acquaintance with the minister and so he got angry and ensured the director was sacked.

Identify a fine lady and initiate moves to get her permission to marry her. They will tell you your home town is too far if you're from the north but they are ready to say yes to somebody from Tuvalu, a place they have not even heard of, or Australia which is a 48-hour flight from Ghana!

If you don't love your own who will love you?

If your laws are rigid towards your citizens but flexible

towards foreigners, what have you achieved? You are just a slave with a colonial mentality.

Let us be fair in the application of our laws. Foreigners must not spit on our laws. As Kublai Khan said, '*This is my country and these are my laws, anyone who will not obey my laws can leave my country.*'

We can't set the laws aside for the betterment of foreigners when we are not willing to do same for our own citizens. Ghana is for Ghanaians, let that sink in." – (Sylvanus Akorsu, "Ghana, the Country That Hates Its Citizens," *Modern Ghana*, 11 November 2019).

When those who have power despise their own people and favour foreigners, usually whites; when they ignore or neglect them as if they don't even exist, they not only help to sustain the belief – propagated by our conquerors – that imperial subjugation of Africans was justified because it was a blessing to them as members of the "lesser breed"; they do irreparable damage to the African psyche among a large number of them who end up believing everything negative that is taught about us including the lie that we are no more than hewers of wood and drawers of water for members of other races, not just whites.

The belief that whites are superior to us is prevalent across the African continent even among some of our leaders although they won't admit that. Not every African believes we are inferior to whites but many do, demonstrated by their glorification and imitation of almost everything white.

There are even some facilities which are reserved almost exclusively for whites. The indigenous people are discouraged from using them, in *their own* country, of *all* places, on spurious grounds – that they are for "tourists," for "our guests," meaning all whites, *any* white. They may not even be allowed to go inside; and if they are, whites are served first and given other preferences in terms of service.

And many whites, as well as other non-blacks, don't have the slightest fear of being punished when they insult black people in our countries.

It goes on in my home country, Tanzania, and it goes on in other parts of Africa, with regular frequency, including post-apartheid South Africa, once the bastion of white supremacy on the continent. As Professor Richard Schroeder, writing about what he witnessed in Tanzania, states in a preface to his book, *Africa after Apartheid: South Africa, Race, and Nation in Tanzania*:

"During my first trip to northern Tanzania in December 1995, my wife and I were invited to a dinner party at the home of some friends. The day of the party was crystal clear, the majestic peaks of Mount Meru and Mount Kilimanjaro emerging from the clouds to provide a spectacular backdrop.

We arrived early and sat outside in a small circle of chairs, drinking beer and enjoying the pleasant weather. Most of the guests were, like us, white expatriates, but they included at least one mixed European/Tanzanian couple. It was a lazy, laid-back affair.

After an hour or so, a white South African who worked for a safari company based in the nearby city of Arusha dropped in uninvited and joined us for a drink. The subject of the ensuing conversation escapes me now, but I do remember how this man repeatedly and unselfconsciously used the racial slur 'kaffir' in reference to Tanzanians. While this term was widely used in South Africa to refer to blacks during the apartheid years, I was shocked to hear it used in Arusha. This was not because this particular *individual* used it – but because he seemed to feel so comfortable using it in *Tanzania*, a country that was one of the staunchest opponents to apartheid.

The implication was that in polite, white expatriate gatherings in northern Tanzania, calling locals 'kaffirs' was an acceptable form of speech.

Since I was new to the area, I wondered how widespread this practice was. Was I correct in thinking that it was out of place in Tanzania? Were others at the party similarly offended by this man? What would Tanzanians make of this situation?

I was aware that this safari operator was one of thousands of white South Africans who relocated to Tanzania and other parts of the continent in pursuit of new business opportunities after the democratic elections that brought Nelson Mandela to power in Pretoria in 1994, but I was unclear whether his behavior was an exception or the rule. The historic post-apartheid encounter between South Africans and the rest of the continent certainly bore watching.

As it turns out, I may have gotten my story about the dinner party wrong: my wife also vividly recalls the conversation I described above, but she places it at the home of another couple entirely; I may have conflated the memories of two different parties in my reconstruction of the event.

This disparity might not be wroth mentioning, except that it led me, years later, to ask both couples if they could identify the South African in question. While none of the four hosts specifically remembered the conversation that day, each couple readily named an individual who they thought might have been responsible for the racist comments. This was striking in tsi own right.

Another long-time resident of northern Tanzania reinforced the notion that South Africans had brought about a change in social mores in Tanzania when I showed her a draft of this preface during a brief visit to Arusha in 2011. After reading the first few paragraphs, she turned to me and said, 'This is not about my house, is it?' When I assured her that it was not, she continued, 'Because it could be. We all know someone like that. The only question, I suppose, is whether we are all talking about the same person.'

Clearly the dinner party guest's behavior in 1995 was not an isolated event....I often found myself in positions where I observed insensitive behavior or overheard offensive speech." – (Richard A. Schroeder, *Africa after Apartheid: South Africa, Race, and Nation in Tanzania*, Bloomington, Indiana, USA: Indiana University Press, pp. ix – x).

The racist behaviour of South African whites Professor Schroeder observed in Tanzania is not unique to this group in the East African country and in other parts of the continent. Many other whites have the same attitude towards black Africans.

This racist stereotype is reinforced by blacks themselves when they don't do as well as whites and other non-blacks do in a number of areas, thus validating the racist notion that black people "just can't help it." They are short on grey matter and it not their fault; they are not endowed by nature with the same mental faculties members of other races are.

And we seem to fail or perform poorly in almost every field of human endeavour because of colonial mentality which fosters the belief that white people – and others – are better than we are, and we have to look to them for inspiration and guidance in order for them to teach us instead of taking the initiative ourselves to learn on our own.

They even come – all the way from Europe and America – to teach us about our own environment including the kinds of animals and plants we have when we should be – and *are* – masters of our own environment. They even come to teach us our own history which we should know more than they do.

There is a persistent belief among many Africans that because the teachers are white, they are better than our own teachers just as many of them have been brainwashed into believing that white doctors are better than black doctors; white engineers and lawyers are better than black engineers and lawyers. The list goes on and on.

All that is a result of colonial mentality – since the advent of colonial rule – and fortifies white supremacy with the help of black people themselves.

Many of our people have lost self-confidence because of that. They think they are inferior to whites and to members of other races; therefore they cannot perform well in many, if not all, areas. They have to wait to be taught or have things done for them by more intelligent people who are invariably members of other races, especially whites. They are also the only ones who can build our economies and therefore develop our countries – for us. We cannot do it ourselves. How can we, "intellectually inferior" as we are?

Some of our people really believe that. We have the unenviable distinction of being the most "backward" people in the world. Even college kids from Europe and America have to come and dig water wells for us and teach us simple hygiene including the necessity of having and using latrines – about which we already know. They even teach us about ventilation and how important it is to let smoke out of our huts and houses when we are cooking or burning wood to stay warm when it is cold.

Even when we are in a position to bring about fundamental change, because of the power we have in our own countries, we sometimes fail or refuse to do so if we think whatever we may do will affect whites and foreigners in a negative way. We don't want to upset them; they come first, our people last, in terms of protecting them and preserving their interests including their status quo – which never changed even after the end of colonial rule and, in the case of South Africa, after the end of apartheid.

And that is where one of the most disturbing examples of colonial mentality comes from, in spite of the political power black people have had in the post-apartheid era for more than 25 years.

Black leaders are still trapped in the past – so are many of their supporters – because of their colonial mentality. As Mosibudi Mangena, former president of the Azania People's Organisation (AZAPO) which fought against apartheid and later became a political party in South Africa, who also was a cabinet member under President Thabo Mbeki, states in his book, *Triumphs and Heartaches: A Courageous Journey by South African Patriots*:

"The colonial mentality is manifestly prevalent in our country. Everywhere you look, you are confronted by evidence of this malady. And colonial mentality or, to put it another way, an inferiority complex, is an affliction that prevents people from behaving confidently and in their own interests.

I believe it is one of the factors contributing to our difficulties to succeed and progress.

How come, 20 years after the attainment of democracy, with political, legislative and executive powers in our hands, we are still singing songs about whites taking our land? Why don't we use the power we have to right the wrong? It is excruciatingly painful to watch ourselves, more often than not led by our people in state executive authority, singing: *"Thina sizwe esimnyama/ Sikhalela izwe lethu/ Elathathwa ngamabhunu/ Maba wuyekele/ Umhlaba wethu* ...(We the black nation/ Are crying for our country/ That was taken by the Boers/ Let them leave it/ Our land ..."

It is so jarring.

Instead of using the power we have to correct the situation, we continue to wail and moan about our seized land.

There are those who say the singing of these melancholic melodies is merely a cultural expression, a reminder of where we come from, but this is patently untrue. Yes, we are known for our singing for every occasion but, ironically, therein lies the answer.

We have songs to express our sorrow about oppression, to rally us for war, to celebrate weddings and for funerals. Every song has a context. We don't sing a funeral song at a wedding. Why would we sing about our seized land if the song does not express our feelings at this point in time? What are the masses supposed to do when their leaders cry and moan, instead of going about solving the problems?

And yet land seizure from Africans by the white colonialists is the main source of African poverty, powerlessness, misery and indignity. It explains why, rightly, all three liberation movements emphasised land restoration as an important goal of the struggle for freedom.

Hence the dismay and exasperation on the part of many of us with the lack of urgency over land reform.

After the attainment of democracy and accepting that there would be no seizure of power in South Africa by the liberation movement, the Azanian People's Organisation (Azapo) proposed three methods to advance land reform, which may be used in concert or separately.

First, it asserted that land expropriation with or without compensation should be pursued. There is nothing, except colonial mentality, stopping us from following this route. The Constitution provides for the expropriation of land to advance the national interest or common good.

Righting the wrongs of the past that continue to wound the majority of the population should be the noblest goal for a democratic government led by a liberation movement. This is so critical that we should not brook any obstacle to it. Even if the Constitution were a problem, we should not hesitate to amend it. After all, it was not made by God, but by us.

Second, those landowners who wish to sell their land to the state to advance land reform should be allowed to do so on a willing-seller, willing-buyer basis. The state should evaluate the property and, all else being equal, acquire it.

Third, the state should impose a tax on land over a specified size and the proceeds should be used to pay for land for reform, especially for the willing-seller, willing-buyer option.

Colonialists did not pussyfoot around when it came to the question of land. They went straight for it, either directly through the barrel of a gun or through cohesive legislative measures. That created the current situation in which land ownership, occupation and utilisation, in both rural and urban areas, favours the white minority so unfairly. This has been an important element in the imbalance of wealth between black and white people for centuries.

One would have imagined that 20 years after democracy, the process of identifying black people who would like to farm on a large scale would have been fairly advanced. Such people would have been settled on suitable land and given all the assistance to succeed, as it is done all over the world.

That policy would have been pursued together with the sentimental one, where forcefully removed communities would be given their land back or financially compensated.

We are not alone in placing land at the centre of our struggle for freedom. The tragic conflict between the Palestinians and Israelis is about land and nationhood – two sides of the same coin. The delay in land reform in Zimbabwe, which similarly centred its liberation struggle on land conquest, led to avoidable and unnecessary social and political strife. There are those among us who keep telling the nation that the Zimbabwe scenario will not occur in South Africa, but I fail to see why not, if we continue to drag our feet on land reform.

For twisted ideological reasons, the white minority regime provided poor education to black people. But black people are now in charge of the education system, in terms of the budget, administration and curriculum. Yet black children are now getting the worst education ever, not in terms of the curriculum or per capita spending, but in terms of effort and application by black adults.

To what would we ascribe this situation and attitude if not self-hate and a colonial mentality? We know black people can teach. They have taught many of us ably in the past under very difficult circumstances. But you will not do the best for your people if you have poor self-evaluation.

It is the same colonial mentality that gives us shocking horrors such as Marikana. The white minority found it easy and acceptable to massacre Africans every now and then, as they did in Sharpeville and Soweto. Ideologically and subliminally, they could justify it.

But what justification do we have for a black government massacring its own people? Neither the government nor the miners own the mines or the platinum produced there. But the workers' own government, through the police, mowed them down with automatic weapons, while the owners of the mines are sitting pretty somewhere abroad, completely safe.

Can any of us imagine the British police massacring British mineworkers with machine guns over a South African-owned mine? It is unthinkable. They would not do it even over a British-owned mine. That is not their mentality. They do not find the lives of their people so expendable.

It is clear we have a deep-seated psychological problem that prevents us from valuing ourselves, our people and our interests. We are a middle-income country that is blessed with considerable natural resources. If we were to use these to provide our nation with a proper and credible education system, medical care and other such services, we would be much further than we are now." – (Mosibudi Mangena, *Triumphs and Heartaches: A Courageous Journey by South African Patriots*, Picado

Africa – Macmillan Publishers, South Africa, 2015; an excerpt from the book reprinted as Mosibudi Mangena, "Self-hate Lies at the Root of Our Difficulties," *Mail&Guardian*, South Africa, 10 April 2015).

We have even failed – after the end of colonial rule – to use the power we have to correct injustices and improve living conditions of our people; our leaders being one of the biggest problems we face in trying to bring about fundamental change that is desperately needed in our countries.

Our dismal performance in the economic arena alone, as others forge ahead, is one of the most humiliating, virtually setting us apart from the rest of mankind, although this is mainly attributed to bad leadership more than anything else, compounded by corruption. But it still reinforces the notion that we are not as good as other people are; they are *all* better than we are.

Yet we can do better, far better than we have done so far, because there is nothing inherently wrong with us which prevents us from doing that.

The sharp contrast between Africans and Asians, shown below, in terms of performance in the economic arena illustrates this point.

Look at the southeast Asian nations which won independence around the same time we did and were colonised just as we were, also around the same time and by the same European powers except in the case of Indonesia. And look at where they are today in sharp contrast with us, complementing and fuelling their success with their own innovations instead of relying – exclusively as we do – on imported knowledge in the scientific and technological fields.

Also, look at Japan which has remained Japanese in all its essential attributes without compromising its identity and heritage in spite of what it has learned so much from the West in terms of science and technology complemented with its own innovations and other means derived from indigenous knowledge to become a highly industrialised nation and a world economic power.

Now look at us, on a continent endowed with an abundance of of natural resources more than any other part of the world; a continent where millions of people want to be more European and American than African, as traditional Africa – with its indigenous knowledge and institutions, values, customs and traditions – is fast receding into the past and colonial mentality continues to take its toll stunting and suffocating African intellectual growth. As I state in one of my books, *Africa is in a Mess: What Went Wrong and What Should Be Done*:

"Since independence in the sixties, Africa has performed poorly in most areas because of bad leadership and bad policies, not because of weak genes.

Most countries on the continent won independence by 1968. Yet, an entire generation later, they have little to show for all those years they have ruled themselves. No one expects a country to develop in 30 or 40 years. But no one expects it to do nothing either. There is no excuse for the kind of economic retardation that has taken place in most countries across Africa since independence. A generation is not a week. When compared with other parts of the developing world, Africa has performed miserably in every conceivable way. And statistics tell the story, a sad story.

In 1965, Nigeria was richer than Indonesia, and Ghana richer than Thailand. Today Indonesia is three times richer than Nigeria, and Thailand five times richer than Ghana.

In 1965, Uganda was richer than South Korea. And in 1967, Zambia also was richer than South Korea. Zambia had a per capita income of $200, and South Korea, $120. After 30 years, South Korea's gross domestic product per person was more than $10,000 in 1998, and Zambia's $400.[4] Yet, by African standards, Zambia is considered to be one of the richest countries on the continent in spite of all the misery, hunger and starvation ravaging this country endowed with abundant minerals and arable land more than enough to feed its entire population.

And all African countries combined have a smaller gross domestic product than that of Belgium, a country of only 10 million people, and one of the smallest in the world. By contrast, Africa's population is more than 700 million on a continent endowed with abundant natural resources.

The gross domestic product of African countries is not only smaller but a mere fraction of Belgium's. What is even more depressing is that Indonesia, a developing country which in 1965 was poorer than Nigeria, has a bigger gross domestic product than that of all the black African countries combined. Yet, Indonesia itself was a colony like the African countries and won independence roughly around the same time that African countries did during the post-World War II era.

It is just as sad, probably even more so, when we look at the dismal performance of black Africa from another perspective. There are 40 black African countries out of 53 on the entire continent which includes the island nations of Madagascar, Mauritius, the Comoros, and the Seychelles, all on the Indian Ocean; Cape Verde, and Sao Tome & Principe on the Atlantic.

More than half of the gross domestic product of the black African countries is contributed by only two countries: South Africa and Nigeria. That means a total of 38 black African countries - almost the entire sub-Saharan region - have a combined gross domestic product which is only about a third of Indonesia's.

And the devastating impact of AIDS, civil wars and corruption makes things worse, much worse, with no relief in sight. Now, an increasing number of people across Africa are turning to churches calling for divine intervention to alleviate their plight.

Something is wrong, terribly wrong. But unlike in the past when it was fashionable for many Africans to blame colonialism and imperialism for almost all the problems our countries faced after we won independence, an increasing number of them today, especially those of the younger generation, insist on accountability within Africa itself as they apportion guilt accordingly; instead of blaming colonialists and imperialists for the perpetual misery - thanks to tyranny, corruption, poverty and disease - hundreds of millions of Africans have to endure all their lives.

To these millions, independence has remained an abstract ideal without any concrete benefits in their lives as they remain trapped in poverty and continue to be ravaged by disease while billions of dollars in foreign aid and taxes paid by the toiling masses are being stolen and squandered by unscrupulous politicians and bureaucrats together with their cronies and mistresses. It is clear where the problem lies. It lies within, not without." – (Godfrey Mwakikagile, *Africa is in a Mess: What Went Wrong and What Should Be Done*, New Africa Press, 2006, pp. 12 – 14).

We have to assume full responsibility for our condition even when we have legitimate complaints against our former conquerors and other outsiders who exploit us. In most cases, they are able to do so only because we allow them to use us.

We even allow and help them to keep us divided because of our colonial mentality.

Colonial mentality has played a major role in keeping Africa divided. And it continues to do so. The divisive and destructive nationalism prevalent across the continent is a product of that. We glorify our countries or nation states, which are a product of imperial rule, at the expense of African unity which can be achieved on regional and continental basis.

We talk about the sanctity of borders we inherited at independence as if we cannot move beyond that in pursuit of higher goals we can achieve in a spirit of Pan-African solidarity.

We rail against imperialism yet are proud of what we inherited from our imperial rulers when they "left." That includes not only institutions of authority, hence states, but also our national identities which are a product of demarcation – the colonial boundaries they drew to create the countries we have today. We are more proud of our artificial national identities than we are of our common African identity which existed before even our continent was named "Africa."

Our common heritage – historical, cultural, spiritual, intellectual and philosophical, sharing many things in those areas – united us and gave us a common identity as Africans; hence, "We Africans are not like that"; "We Africans don't do that"; "We Africans respect older people, including older brothers and sisters and others, not just elders;" "That is not how we see the world"; "We are united by our humanity," and so on.

We did not have a common name for our continent. Our common identity was its name even without being a name.

A name does not create identity, let alone an identity that already exists as a natural entity, which is what our collective identity is as the indigenous inhabitants of our continent even though it did not have a common name before foreigners named our motherland.

We should ask ourselves serious questions:

What is so sacred in keeping our countries divided along colonial boundaries and killing each another – millions dead, for example, during the Nigerian civil war between secessionist Biafra and Federal Nigeria – just to maintain those boundaries, hence artificial nations, formed by our former colonial masters instead of redrawing them to defuse conflict?

Why can't we draw our own boundaries and redraw the map of Africa to reflect our own realities, African realities, and accommodate the interests of all groups and enable them to ventilate their grievances under new political arrangements agreed upon – all the way down to the grassroots level – by all those involved in different parts of the continent?

Who said Uganda is sacred? Who said Niger, Zambia, Nigeria, Congo, Cameroon, Ghana are untouchable simply because our former conquerors said they should exist that way?

Why are we so proud of the imperial creations – Kenya, Guinea, Malawi, Sierra Leone, Mali and so on?

We did not have them before our conquerors came. That does mean we did not exist until they came. We did not ask them to name us and define us. But they did and told us from now on you are so-and-so – Rhodesian, Ugandan, Tanganyikan, Nigerian, Sierra Leonean, Togolese, and so forth.

This also led to a division of natural resources on the basis of colonial borders, resources which were shared before our colonial rulers came.

What was once ours, together, now belongs to them, across the border. The people, including families, found themselves separated by colonial boundaries. They were no longer one people and even became enemies in some cases. Conflicts which never existed before became a reality because of colonial boundaries.

"You belong over there, across the border, and we belong over here. You are a Kenyan and I am a Tanganyikan."

"Who said so?" "The British, our colonial masters, who named us Kenyans and Tanganyikans. They gave us separate new identities. We are different people."

We even fight over land and water we shared before our European rulers came and divided us and created new countries defined by colonial borders.

Look at the dispute between Malawi and Tanzania over Lake Nyasa. Malawians call it Lake Malawi. Tanzanians call it Lake Nyasa.

I come from that area. My home village, north of Kyela in Kyela District, is only about 30 miles from the Tanzanian-Malawian border. I come from Rungwe District.

Members of my own ethnic group were forcibly divided and separated by this arbitrary demarcation following the partition of Africa sanctioned by the imperial powers at the Berlin Conference in 1885. They are called Nyakyusa on our side of the border in Tanzania and Ngonde across the border in Malawi. Yet they are one and the same people.

Before the colonial boundaries were drawn, the lake belonged to all the people in the area. But after colonial borders were formed, the boundaries placed the lake on the side of Nyasaland, as Malawi was known during British colonial rule. But the British also, who ruled both countries – Tanganyika and Nyasaland – had both countries share the lake and even had some maps showing the boundary between the two countries was in the middle of the lake. I remember using those maps when I was in primary school in the late 1950s. The British named the lake – Lake Nyasa.

Now the people of Malawi say the lake is exclusively theirs; the people on the other side of the border in Tanzania have no legitimate claim to it because it is no longer theirs, thanks to the colonial boundaries we inherited at independence.

We don't have enough sense to say we are still the *same* people – one people – and the lake belongs to us all. We sometimes say that but don't mean it in concrete terms; we don't practise what we say.

Colonial boundaries don't have to turn us into rivals or enemies when we weren't before. They should even be an incentive for us to unite – break down those barriers and form larger political entities transcending narrow and petty nationalism.

Let Malawi and Tanzania unite under a federal government or form a confederation and the lake will be ours together again, as before, even though we did not have such large political units then in the region.

It is a tragedy that we still cherish what our former colonial rulers left behind even when it does not serve our collective interests as fellow Africans.

That is one of the worst legacies of colonial rule, reinforced by colonial mentality which has many Africans glorifying things European, including their capacity to divide us on the basis of colonial borders although we are one people.

We have made some progress. But in spite of the strides we have made since independence to make our sovereign status a reality, we still have a long way to go. We won political independence in the legal sense – at least flag independence. But we have not achieved true mental liberation. Colonial mentality still pervades the land.

It is a problem that we are going to have for a long time, as many of our people desperately try to run away from themselves and become what they are not, aping European ways of life and consumption proclivities of the West. They are ashamed of their African heritage and ways of life and even their identity as Africans.

They are not even aware of the negative and devastating psychological impact colonial rule has had on the minds of Africans for generations. They take the opposite view. They believe colonial rule was beneficial and shaped the minds of Africans in a positive way.

The reality is colonial rule was not beneficial except superficially in terms of material civilisation which fades into insignificance when contrasted with its negative impact on its victims including loss of countless lives.

Yet, we must also acknowledge that few of us would

want to destroy the infrastructure – the most visible symbol of Western material civilisation in Africa – built by the colonial rulers simply because it was a product of imperial rule. And hardly any of us would say colonial rulers should never have built schools, clinics, and hospitals and other facilities as well as different kinds of institutions in our countries which we inherited at independence

All those facilities and institutions were also beneficial to us in varying degrees before independence. And we continued to use them after we won independence. Still, they were collectively an infrastructure of conquest – as all colonial institutions were – intended to facilitate and consolidate imperial rule and domination of the indigenous people. The primary purpose of building roads and railways as well as other infrastructure was not to help Africans but to help Europeans. And Africans were ruthlessly exploited to sustain the colonial states. As Professor Crawford Young states in his book, *The Postcolonial State in Africa: Fifty Years of Independence, 1960 – 2010*:

"Metropolitan treasuries demanded that the new territorial domains be self-financing: in most areas, sustenance for the colonial occupation could only be generated from the newly subjugated African through taxation, obligatory labor for the state, or muscular recruitment to work European mines and plantations. This in turn necessitated the construction of a frugal but brutal command state, with a thin layer of European agents operating through a denser network composed of chiefly intermediaries and indigenous armed auxiliaries.

The establishment of the colonial state coincided with the historical zenith of virulent racism, which permeated government policy reason with a premise of African inferiority. 'African culture,' I wrote, for the colonizer 'had no redeeming value; only a wholly new African might be worthy of the colonial order, tailored from imported cloth'....

The mentalities, routines, and quotidian modes of operation....[from] the African colonial state...were inevitably embedded in the postcolonial successor states, lodged within a legacy of autocratic practice." – (Crawford Young, *The Postcolonial State in Africa: Fifty Years of Independence, 1960 – 2010*, Madison, Wisconsin, USA: The University of Wisconsin Press, 2012, p. 6. See also Crawford Young, *The African Colonial State in Comparative Perspective*, New Haven, Connecticut, USA: Yale University Press, 1994).

The colonial rulers wanted to create "a new African" who was compliant, submissive, throughly brainwashed and whitewashed, and ready to accept and glorify imperial rule and white civilisation.

They, as members of "the advanced race" – to use William Buckley's term when he defended racial segregation against blacks in the United States, not just in the south – even wanted Africans to accept and ignore racial subjugation because it was an integral part of their civilising mission among the natives who were "savages" and "backward" in every conceivable way and in the lower echelons of the racial hierarchy; some of them "lower" than others, according to the colonial rulers, for example, the Tutsi being in the higher echelon than the Hutu, a classification that was a vital part of their policy of divide and rule.

Yet, out of sheer necessity and – thanks to colonial mentality – even with some pride in what we inherited from our colonial rulers, we used the *same* colonial infrastructure and institutions to build our countries after we won independence, adapting them to suit our needs.

This is not a defence of colonial rule – it is simply an acknowledgement of reality, however harsh and offensive it may be to our nationalist sensibilities.

Colonial rule even helped to forge ties and facilitated interaction between members of different tribes or ethnic groups. Many of them did not know about each other until colonial rulers came and brought them together as fellow citizens of the countries formed by the colonialists. Some of them did not even know about the existence of other tribes beyond their neighbours.

Members of different tribes also got the chance to know each other when they attended the same schools – founded by the colonial rulers and by the missionaries – and when they worked together for the colonial government in different parts of the country; interactions which also played a role in nation building during and after colonial rule by breaking down tribal or ethnic barriers – in spite of the colonial rulers' policy of divide-and-rule.

Colonial rule, however offensive and predatory, also played a major role in introducing us to each other as individuals and as tribes or ethnic groups and even as independence movements or anticolonial agitators.

Imperial rule even helped create a sense of nationalism and solidarity among Africans in different parts of the continent and on a continental scale. It brought them together – united them against a common enemy – and was a major catalyst in nationalist agitation across the continent. As Julius Nyerere stated:

"Africans all over the continent, without a word being spoken either from one individual to another, or from one country to another, looked at the European, looked at one another, and knew that in relation to the European they were one." – (Julius Nyerere, in Godfrey Mwakikagile, *Africa and the West*, Huntington, New York: Nova Science Publishers, 2000, p. 70).

Modern African countries were built on the foundations laid by the colonial rulers. And it was the colonial rulers who determined the shape and personality of our countries. The task for us is to change that personality and make it authentically African.

Colonial rule left a complex legacy even though its positive aspects or modernising influence on traditional – hence "backward" – societies cannot be used to justify its existence. Modernisation, however positive in many respects, weakened and even destroyed traditional institutions which served Africans very well before the advent of colonial rule and should not have been replaced by institutions brought by Europeans.

The most devastating and long-lasting impact of colonial rule was psychological. It corrupted and distorted the minds of Africans, in fact, so much so that many of them, even decades after independence, have unwittingly become agents of imperial domination of our continent, helping to perpetuate it.

They believe the destiny of Africa is inextricably linked with the destiny of Europe and America, for our own benefit, and therefore maintaining and strengthening ties with the metropolitan powers is vital for our own well-being and prosperity because they care about us. They don't see it as an asymmetrical relationship tipping scales in favour of the imperial powers to the detriment of Africa's well-being.

Colonial mentality has blinded many Africans to reality. Even when our former colonial masters – and others – do to us what they are not supposed to do, at our expense and to our detriment, many Africans deliberately overlook or ignore that or say there is nothing wrong with it. Our former imperial masters are "always right" because they brought us up "the right way" under colonial tutelage.

But there are even some Africans of the younger generation who are fully aware of the problem and the negative impact colonial mentality has had and continues to have on Africa's well-being and integrity. As Oluwatubi

Odeyinka, who was a student at Moshood Abiola Polytechnic in Abeokuta, Nigeria, stated in his article, "Colonial Mentality in All of Us," in a Nigerian newspaper, *The Nation*:

"It is not out of place to state emphatically that most Nigerians, if not all, are white men in black skins, as we have projected ourselves as promoters of the customs, beliefs, lifestyles and conventions of our colonial masters.

Before I broach the subject matter, let me disclose that I was inspired to write on this topic by two incidents. The first was a fierce argument on the Champions League final between Real Madrid and Liverpool, while the other was an embarrassing slavery scene of a Chinese construction company, conveying their black labourers in a manner similar to the slave trade era.

I watched with keen interest how hardworking Nigerian youths engaged in passionate debate about the Champions League final. While the fans of Real Madrid boasted about the unmatched experience of the Spanish team in the competition; those that comprised supporters of especially English teams pledged their support for Liverpool.

However, the sympathisers of Liverpool, I perceived, were only in solidarity walk with the team so that the true fans do not walk alone as they tackled almighty Madrid last May. The ones I identified as supporters of Chelsea, Arsenal, and Manchester United pledged their support for Liverpool on the premise that it is an English team.

'We are loyal to EPL,' one of them said.

'Really,' I muttered. When did an EPL team become Enugu Rangers or Sunshine Stars of Ibadan to deserve our loyalty?

I subjected my brain to rigorous exercise and I resolve that, the self-infected colonial mentality seems hereditary – our forefathers had a taste of colonial yoke during the years of colonial rule and the ambience of colonialism has refused to depart successive generations. Despite being granted independence on October 1, 1960, we still project ourselves to be offshoots to world powers like our very own Great Britain, United States of America (USA), France, and others.

I would not wish to go into political and economic neo-colonialism, a contraption standing against the progress of most African countries, but I shall limit this discourse to deliberate on the traits of colonialism in our society....

Colonial mentality...is an attitude of ethnic or cultural inferiority that has found its way into our subconscious existence and unashamedly seems to be eroding our traditional culture. I shall soon get to the second incident I witnessed, and readers would agree with me that Fela was right when he said: '*dem don release you now, but you never release yourself...*'

Apart from supporting European football teams, do we not also crave for imported goods? Nigerians define class by foreign appearance. They want to know from what country you got your shirts, which foreign company produced your shoes, and which foreign brand sell the smartest suits?

Our wild appetite for foreign products is legendary. Those in the top echelon of the society join the government in preaching 'buy made-in-Nigeria products,' yet they rush to buy foreign products. Isn't that an attestation to colonial mentality?

As a man, when assessing a lady, you consider European features to be the standard for beauty; you detest our traditional hairstyles like *kolese, kojusoko, ipako-elede*, but prefer Ghana weavings, Russian style or Brazilian braids. What has happened to an '*Omoluabi*' appearance?

The height of inferiority complex is the use of bleaching cream. Those bleaching their skin prefer the artificial coke and Fanta colour it gives to their natural dark skin. Some of them bleach their skins and turn out to be worst humans.

Most annoying are those who discriminate against their fellow countrymen in such areas as class, religion and ethnicity. The way Nigerians have personalised and indigenised the foreign religions is amazing; 'black folks can tell you about every religion under the sun, but too sacred to talk about their own African gods.'

Favouring traditional European attires (suits) over our own *kembe* for formal occasions is an evidence that we are comfortable being subservient to our colonial masters. About two weeks ago, one of my friends, Kenny, was clad in *Ankara* material and he was being queried by his classmates why he would appear native on a Monday. He wondered if it was in the school regulation not to wear native attires on a Monday. Kenny was being scrutinised as though, he was mentally ill, simply because he dropped the colonial convention.

About the Chinese construction company that I mentioned earlier, it is pathetic and dehumanising scene which made me feel ashamed of my fatherland.

Every day, I see Nigerians working with China Civil Engineering Construction Corporation (CCECC) being lumped together like sardine fishes at the back of pick-up vehicles to and from construction sites, while the expatriate contractors are ridden in posh vehicles with tinted glasses and police cover.

For how long would our graduates be doing menial jobs under foreigners like their fathers did last century, while the expatriates with college certificates get government contracts all in the name of 'technical experts?'

Nigerian leaders are so in awe of expatriates that even in things as mundane as road constructions. Our leaders take pride in being photographed with some second rate foreign contractors. These contractors, I'm sure, are not different from illiterate bricklayers we have here, but the

Chinese contractors will be parading themselves as the best professionals in the face of our leaders.

Colonial mentality has eaten deep our brain and its pervasiveness is easily noticed. We are a people who feel inferior of originality in a bid to glorify foreigners and their concepts. When will Nigerians purge themselves of this colonial mentality?" – (Oluwatubi Odeyinka, "Colonial Mentality in All of Us," in a Nigerian newspaper, *The Nation*, 30 August 2018; also published in *Campus Life*, Moshood Abiola Polytechnic, Abeokuta, Nigeria, 30 August 2018).

It is not just Nigerians – the question is continental in scope: When will Africans purge themselves of this colonial mentality?

Many Africans really believe that we cannot develop without begging other people to help us, a belief which is a product of imperial subjugation, rooted in colonial mentality. Yet no country has ever developed by depending on other people. Still, we continue to beg them to help us. We beg too much – always *for something*.

As we reflect on our successes and failures, and as we chart out a new course into the future in this selfish world where those who thrive are concerned about their own well-being more than they are about the well-being of others; and in a world where power respects *only* power and is impressed by nothing less; we should realise that our future as a people and the destiny of Africa as a continent cannot depend on the guidance, benevolence and ingenuity of others. We must look within to reawaken the giant that is in us and take giant steps forward and into a future only we can and *must* control for our own well-being. We don't have to follow in the footsteps of others.

Look within, not without, for inspiration and guidance. Our ancestors may have been wrong in many things but they were not wrong in everything. Whatever knowledge they bequeathed us must be used to secure and promote our own well-being instead of *always* ignoring it in preference of what comes from outside Africa. We can use both but only when there *is* a need to do so. They can complement each other.

We should look within ourselves for solutions to our problems, solutions derived from indigenous knowledge and local circumstances determined by the conditions which prevail in our societies, complemented by what we learn from interacting with other people – as much as they learn from us for their own well-being – in an interdependent world but which is also not as compassionate as some of our people think it is.

We have a rich heritage which can guide us into the future. Unfortunately, many of our people continue to lose their true African identity, a tragedy that began with colonisation which is synonymous with Westernisation. Westernisation itself is synonymous with "civilisation," a definition that is accepted by many of our people and which largely explains why so many of them still have colonial mentality, glorifying our conquerors who came from the West. It is a form of psychological bondage which has had a devastating impact on Africa's well-being and destiny.

There is an imperative need to purge our minds of ideas and thoughts which diminish us as human beings before the rest of the world and which foster a mentality that other people are better than we are in terms of intellect and in every other conceivable way.

That is something that should be done even before we start harnessing our full potential which is enormous and is derived from our rich and diverse heritage in all areas of life stretching back into antiquity. That is the Africa that *is* Africa.

Unfortunately, true African renaissance has hardly begun.

Appendix

Berlin 1884:
Remembering the conference
that divided Africa

Patrick Gathara
Aljazeera.com
15 November 2019

135 years ago today, European leaders sat around a horseshoe-shaped table to set the rules for Africa's colonisation.

On the afternoon of Saturday, November 15, 1884, an international conference was opened by the chancellor of the newly-created German Empire at his official residence on Wilhelmstrasse, in Berlin. Sat around a horseshoe-shaped table in a room overlooking the garden with representatives from every European country, apart from Switzerland, as well as those from the United States and the Ottoman Empire.

The only clue as to the purpose of the November gathering of white men was hung on the wall – a large map of Africa "drooping down like a question mark" as

Nigerian historian, Professor Godfrey Uzoigwe, would comment.

Including a short break for Christmas and the New Year, the West African Conference of Berlin would last 104 days, ending on February 26, 1885.

In the 135 years since, the conference has come to represent the late 19th-century European Scramble and Partition of the continent. In the popular imagination, the delegates are hunched over a map, armed with rulers and pencils, sketching out national borders on the continent with no idea of what existed on the ground they were parcelling out. Yet this is mistaken.

The Berlin Conference did not begin the scramble. That was well under way. Neither did it partition the continent. Only one state, the short-lived horror that was the Congo Free State, came out of it – though strictly speaking it was not actually a creation of the conference.

It did something much worse, though, with consequences that would reverberate across the years and be felt until today. It established the rules for the conquest and partition of Africa, in the process legitimising the ideas of Africa as a playground for outsiders, its mineral wealth as a resource for the outside world not for Africans and its fate as a matter not to be left to Africans.

From the very start, the conference laid out the order of priorities. "The Powers are in the presence of three interests: That of the commercial and industrial nations, which a common necessity compels to the research of new outlets. That of the States and of the Powers summoned to exercise over the regions of the Congo an authority which will have burdens corresponding to their rights. And, lastly, that which some generous voices have already commended to your solicitude – the interests of the native populations."

It also resolutely refused to consider the question of sovereignty, and the legitimacy of laying claim to someone else's land and resources.

Uzoigwe notes that: "Bismarck … stated in his opening remarks that delegates had not been assembled to discuss matters of sovereignty either of African states or of the European powers in Africa."

It was no accident that there were no Africans at the table – their opinions were not considered necessary. The efforts of the Sultan of Zanzibar to get himself invited to the party were summarily laughed off by the British.

American journalist Daniel De Leon described the conference as "an event unique in the history of political science ... Diplomatic in form, it was economic in fact." And it is true that while it was dressed up as a humanitarian summit to look at the welfare of locals, its agenda was almost purely economic.

Few on the continent or in the African diaspora were fooled. A week before it closed, the *Lagos Observer* declared that "the world had, perhaps, never witnessed a robbery on so large a scale."

Six years later, another editor of a Lagos newspaper, comparing the legacy conference to the slave trade, said: "A forcible possession of our land has taken the place of a forcible possession of our person."

Theodore Holly, the first black Protestant Episcopal Bishop in the US, condemned the delegates as having "come together to enact into law, national rapine, robbery and murder."

The outcome of the conference was the General Act signed and ratified by all but one of the 14 nations at the table, the US being the sole exception.

Some of its main features were the establishment of a regime of free trade stretching across the middle of Africa, the development of which became the rationale for the recognition of the Congo Free State and its subsequent 13-year horror, the abolition of the overland slave trade as well as the principle of "effective occupation."

Though the attempt to create a free trade area in Africa and therefore keep the continent from becoming both a spark for, and a theatre of conflict between the European powers, was ultimately doomed.

The principle of "effective occupation" was to become the catalyst for military conquest of the African continent with far-reaching consequences for its inhabitants.

At the time of the conference, 80 percent of Africa remained under traditional and local control. The Europeans only had influence on the coast.

Following it, they started grabbing chunks of land inland, ultimately creating a hodgepodge of geometric boundaries that was superimposed over indigenous cultures and regions of Africa.

However, to get their claims over African land accepted, European states had to demonstrate that they could actually administer the area.

Often, military victory proved to be the easy part. To govern, they found they had to contend with a confusing milieu of fluid identities and cultures and languages.

The Europeans thus set about reorganising Africans into units they could understand and control. As Professor Terence Ranger noted, the colonial period was marked "by systematic inventions of African traditions – ethnicity, customary law, 'traditional' religion. Before colonialism Africa was characterised by pluralism, flexibility, multiple identity; after it, African identities of 'tribe', gender and generation were all bounded by the rigidities of invented tradition."

That first-ever international conference on Africa established a template for how the world deals with the continent. Today, Africa is still seen primarily as a source for raw materials for the outside world and an arena for them to compete over. Conferences about the continent are rarely held on the continent itself and rarely care about the views of ordinary Africans.

The sight of African heads of state assembling in foreign capitals to beg for favours is a re-enactment of the Sultan of Zanzibar's pleading to attend a conference where he would be the main course.

Despite achieving independence for the most part in the 1950s and 1960s, many African countries have continued along the destructive path laid out in Berlin.

Former Tanzanian President Julius Nyerere declared: "We have artificial 'nations' carved out at the Berlin Conference in 1884, and today we are struggling to build these nations into stable units of human society... we are in danger of becoming the most Balkanised continent of the world."

Ethnicity and tribalism continue to be the bane of African politics. "The Berlin Conference was Africa's undoing in more ways than one," wrote Jan Nijman, Peter Muller and Harm de Blij in their book, *Geography: Realms, Regions, and Concepts*. "The colonial powers superimposed their domains on the African continent. By the time independence returned to Africa… the realm had acquired a legacy of political fragmentation that could neither be eliminated nor made to operate satisfactorily."

Now, 135 years after Berlin, it is perhaps time for introspection.

While it is impossible to turn back the clock, Africans would do well to reflect on what has happened since. Teaching the real history of the subjugation of the continent would help counter the myths of "ancient hatreds" that are said to fuel the conflicts on the continent. And Africans could decide to get together on the continent to debate and decide on the relationship they want with the rest of the world rather than always having that dictated to them from abroad.

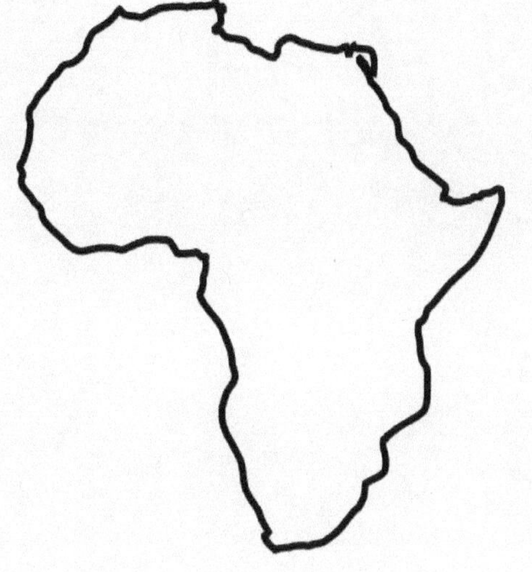